Footprints across Quebec

Footprints across Quebec

The autobiography of
Murray Heron
*—pioneer missionary
to Quebec*

with Ginette Cotnoir

press

Dundas, Ontario

Joshua Press Inc., Dundas, Ontario
fax 905.627.8451 www.joshuapress.com

Reprinted 2001

Editorial director: Michael A.G. Haykin
Creative/production manager: Janice Van Eck

© Cover design by Janice Van Eck
Edited by Ginette Cotnoir

Canadian Cataloguing in Publication Data

Heron, Murray, 1924–
    Footprints across Quebec: the autobiography of Murray Heron—pioneer missionary to Quebec

ISBN 1-894400-01-1

1. Heron, Murray, 1924–   . 2. Evangelistic work – Quebec (Province). 3. Baptists – Quebec (Province) – Clergy – Biography. I. Cotnoir, Ginette. II. Title.

BV3785.H47A3 1999   286'.1714'092   C99-931004-6

To my wife Georgia and my children,
Susan, Joanne, Donald, Janice and Carolyn
who stood faithfully with me during the early years of
evangelism in Quebec and were subsequently used in
many ways as the Lord brought victory and enabled
us to reach thousands of French Canadians
for Jesus Christ

Every place that the sole of your foot will tread upon
I have given you, as I said to Moses.
Joshua 1:3

Contents

Foreword

Murray Heron became my pastor when he came to Église Baptiste Évangélique de Chomedey, Laval, in 1977. His messages were frequently peppered with stories from his early years of ministry in Rouyn-Noranda. Mr. Heron's unassuming manner, his sense of humour and a touch of dramatic flair made his stories memorable. Without fail he brought his listeners to the conclusion that God is powerful and in control of every situation.

After hearing Mr. Heron speak about his pioneer ministry in Quebec, people frequently urged him to put his unique experiences in writing. In 1995, he began recording his recollections on cassettes which I then transcribed and edited. Additional material was gathered from clippings, letters and interviews. Our prayer is that readers will be not only informed but also inspired by this account.

Ginette Cotnoir,
Managing editor, *The Evangelical Baptist*

Acknowledgements

I greatly appreciate the work of Ginette Cotnoir who spent so many hours editing and revising the text. She also did an invaluable task in examining numerous newspaper clippings, news bulletins and personal letters to make this account an accurate historical document without detracting from the excitement of so many interesting stories. The book would not have been possible without her.

I would also like to thank three sisters, Josie Bury, Margaret (Bury) Mikelait and Georgia (Bury) Ludgate who helped my wife and me in our ministry in northwestern Quebec. They contributed valuable firsthand knowledge to the book and numerous useful recommendations in the editing process.

I also want to mention those who carefully read this manuscript before publication and gave us encouragement and helpful suggestions. They include: Lorne and Margaret Heron, Eileen Veals, Verna Cotnoir, Margaret Brouillette, my wife and all my children. I am also grateful for the many others who gave me valuable prayer support.

Murray Heron
Boisbriand, Quebec
March 1999

Introduction

Also I heard the voice of the Lord, saying:
"Whom shall I send,
And who will go for Us?"
Then I said, "Here am I! Send me."
Isaiah 6:8

"Are you big enough to leave your footprints in the sands of time?" The question burned in my heart late one Sunday night in 1948. A most unlikely young man had challenged me with these words earlier that summer evening following an open-air meeting in the twin cities of Rouyn-Noranda.

I was walking home from the meeting place downtown, a piano accordion case in my right hand and a large briefcase full of Bibles and hymnals in the other, when I saw an inebriated man coming in my direction. He was staggering from side to side along the sidewalk. As I wondered how to get by him with my two heavy bags, this complete stranger stopped to talk to me. He said he had attended our street meeting and was impressed to see so many young people participating in the singing and the preaching. He thought Christianity was only for older people and could not understand what attraction it could have for anyone his age. We were only a short distance from the church, so I invited him in to continue our conversation.

I learned that this handsome young man was a mining engineer who had recently graduated from university. I will never forget his hopeless look as we sat in the front pew of the empty church. Yet I sensed his desire to find the true meaning of life. In the quietness of the late hour, I explained to him how Jesus was the answer to the longing in his heart. Sadly, he was in such a state of intoxication that he seemed unable to grasp much of what I said.

His lack of knowledge about the Scriptures became apparent as we spoke, but evidently he wanted to say something that sounded religious. He paraphrased a line from the poetry of Henry Wadsworth Longfellow, asking: "Are you big enough to leave your footprints in the sands of time?" I never heard from this man again, but his question taken from the pages of the past gripped my heart and left me with an extraordinary challenge.

I was then at the beginning of my ministry in the province of Quebec, where millions of people had never heard the message of the gospel of Jesus Christ. Young and inexperienced, I approached my task with fear and trembling. I knew I was not big enough to leave my footprints in the sands of time, so I prayed, "Lord, grant that in your great and infinite mercy, you will leave your footprints across Quebec."

It is my prayer that, as you read this book, you will see how God overcame enormous obstacles and opened doors to reach Quebec with the gospel. The good news was preached through open-air meetings, radio, television, day schools, youth camps, literature sent by mail, personal evangelism and church planting. In the last few decades, many French-Canadians have responded to the call of God to pursue seminary training for the ministry. The Lord has answered *my* prayer and the prayers of countless others in a wonderful way by leaving *his footprints across Quebec.*

1

From the farm to seminary

For you see your calling, brethren,
that not many wise according to the flesh,
not many mighty, not many noble, *are called.*
I Corinthians 1:26

I was born near Toronto in 1924, the fourth son of a family of seven boys and one girl. The Heron family had lived in this area of Canada since the arrival of our ancestors from southwest Scotland in the early nineteenth century. After arriving in New York in 1792, they first settled in Niagara Falls and later travelled by ox cart through the bush to the wilderness of the north shore of Lake Ontario where Toronto stands today. My forefathers were among the early pioneers who cleared the land for farming before the city was established. In memory of those early forebears, there is presently a park and a commercial building in east Toronto bearing the Heron name.

When I was nine years old, my parents, William and Pearl Heron (née Atkinson), bought a farm 25 miles east of Toronto in the fertile environs of what was then the village of Pickering. My father returned to the agricultural life he had known as a boy. It was a time when Canada was in the grips of the Great Depression, and raising a large family was difficult. Life on the farm began at 5:30 in the morning when we were roused from our sleep to go down to the stable to milk the cows and feed the animals. Just as the sun was rising in the eastern sky, my dad led the procession with an oil lantern, followed by my brothers and me trudging behind. Each day was filled with work from dawn till dusk, and each year brought a cycle of planting and harvesting grain, hay and corn, and tending a large vegetable garden.

Despite the hard work, it was a good life. My parents found the time to give us the occasional break, piling us all into the car and taking us a few miles south to the beautiful beaches of Lake Ontario or to the swimming hole at a nearby creek.

(from left) George, Ross, Harold, Murray, Lorne, Isabel, Arnold and Earl Heron. Circa 1937.

We received our elementary education at the little one-room school-house, which stood on the corner of our property. We would run down through the orchard, crawl through the hole in the rickety wire fence, and promptly be seated at our desks. One teacher taught all the students from grade one through high school entrance level.

Mother's faith

The Christian example of my parents had a great impact on me. Their trust in the Lord during difficult times was central to our family life. Every Sunday, without fail, we headed to the same United Church my parents had attended all their lives. My parents had become Christians when they were young and had started attending this church when it was a Methodist Church. Today I realize the magnitude of this weekly undertaking: getting seven boys and one girl cleaned up and ready, crowding the ten of us into the car and then minding a pew full of eight squirming children.

At home, we prayed and read the Scriptures each morning before going to school. At night, it was our custom to gather in the living room with our parents to memorize Bible verses and kneel in prayer. Often we would crowd around the piano to sing as my mother played old gospel hymns.

Sometimes Mom wrote out her prayers. These give a glimpse into the depth of her faith in everyday circumstances.

March 20, 1938

Dear Father in Heaven,
I think of the many, many times in the past when thou did come to me
in need and in answer to prayer and wilt thou come now and save our
cow and calf. Wilt thou bring it through with ease and may everything
go well as thou art so able to make it do, dear Jesus. And hear us Oh
Lord and help us with regard to the money we need to get our car this
week and other money to put us on our feet to pay our many bills, Oh
Father. Do please give us what we need in thy wonderful way.

June 1938

Dear Jesus,
Won't you please come and help us and give us a most successful year,
better than we dare hope for. Our little chickens are dying and the
tomatoes that we have set out look so bad. Won't you Jesus, send us
money in some way that we can invest in more livestock.
*   I do thank you for getting us the money last week for taxes and all*
the wonderful lessons it has taught us.

Despite my parents' devotion, I did not personally accept the Lord as my
Lord and Saviour during my childhood. As a teenager I found church bor-
ing. I had little concern for spiritual matters and eventually stopped
attending services with my family at the United Church. I was fourteen
years old in 1939 when Canada followed Great Britain into World War II.
The war brought major changes, which transformed the appearance of the
country. The terrible economic depression of the previous decade vanished
and there was an abundance of money and jobs.

Although the conflict brought a certain amount of financial relief to our
family, it was accompanied by the grim reality of war itself. I was too young
to enlist but my three older brothers, George, Ross and Harold, were soon
wearing military uniforms. Ross went to the battlefront in Europe, risking
his life on the front lines for four years. This was an anxious time for the
whole family.

During these years, a giant munitions plant was built in rural Pickering
and over 5,000 people came to work in the enormous factory just south of
our farm. Part of the township of Pickering became the city of Ajax, and
the area was flooded with newcomers eager to do their part for the war
effort. Our quiet country orchard was transformed into a busy trailer park.
There were people everywhere.

Along with this large influx came Christian workers from Baptist churches
in Toronto. They preached the gospel in the small schoolhouse next to our

farm. By this time I had finished high school. Because I had no interest in making farming my life profession, I went to Toronto to study business. After graduation, I found work in the office of General Motors in Oshawa. It was a good job, but I felt that something was missing in my life.

At the crossroads of life

Tom Delaney, a friend who was a Christian, invited me to a young people's meeting at the schoolhouse. His vivid interest in spiritual matters surprised me and his insistence persuaded me to accept the invitation. My brother, Lorne, just 15 months my junior, was also invited but he had decided not to go because he wanted to repair his bicycle. Just before the meeting, the Baptist pastor, Rev. Donald Dinnick, came by our farm to encourage us to join them. When he heard about Lorne's problem, he simply took off his jacket and helped him fix the bike. As a result, both Lorne and I attended the meeting that night.

I was greatly touched by the concern and love the young people expressed for me. Sitting at a school desk, I participated in lively gospel singing and listened to a powerful message about the Cross and Christ's sacrifice for me. Pastor Dinnick urged us to make a decision for Christ. Despite my church-going background, this was the first time I was being challenged to respond to the love of God. At that initial meeting, I accepted the invitation and the Lord came into my life, filling a deep, inner void.

When I returned to my job the next day I began to feel the first stirrings of the Lord speaking to me about vocational ministry. This new desire was undoubtedly an answer to my mother's prayers. On a number of occasions, she had expressed quite openly that she felt I was going to be a preacher. I was not fond of this idea, as I had a low opinion of the work of a minister, imagining it to be particularly dull and unexciting. Now, with Christ in my life, the words of my mother came alive and my attitude to Christian service began to change.

Nevertheless I had strong misgivings and I firmly told the Lord there was no possibility I could become a pastor. I felt that public speaking was the last thing I would be able to do. I remembered only too well how I had embarrassed myself in high school when required to stand and read aloud to the class. I was so shy and ill at ease that I lost my breath and finally sat down without completing the reading.

I found myself at a crossroads. Would I continue in the office of General Motors with the guarantee of a good salary for years to come or would I choose the great unknown of full-time service for the Lord? I understand now that the great Lord of the harvest is able to call his servants despite all the excuses and objections they might have. Moses living deep in the desert seemed an unlikely candidate to lead the children of Israel out of Egypt, but he was definitely God's choice. God spoke to him so clearly that Moses knew it was in God's divine plan for him to undertake this enormous task. So it was with me.

When I returned to the young people's meeting the following week, the message was just what I needed to hear. The speaker quoted 1 Corinthians 1:26–27, where the apostle Paul writes: "For you see your calling, brethren, that not many wise according to the flesh, not many mighty, not many noble, *are called*. But God has chosen the foolish things of the world to put to shame the wise, and God has chosen the weak things of the world to put to shame the things which are mighty." These verses of Scripture were just for me and effectively removed all my arguments. I became convinced the Lord wanted me in his service even though I felt I did not have the required abilities.

I began to see evidence of the Holy Spirit's transforming power in my life. I had deep, abiding joy and sensed God's presence as never before. Years earlier, my mother had given me a Bible with the inscription: "I trust you will read a chapter every day" on the flyleaf. But I never did. Now I had a real desire to read God's Word and memorize Scripture. I typed up cards with a verse on one side and the reference on the other and began memorizing these verses during my ten-mile bus ride to work each day.

I also felt an urge to witness to my co-workers. I was excited about my new life in Christ and thought they would all be converted, but my efforts to share the gospel met chiefly with indifference or ridicule. Nonetheless, I had a burden for evangelism, and the desire to share my faith persisted.

The Lord had raised up a zealous group of young people among the congregation that met in the schoolhouse, including my brother Lorne who also came to Christ the same summer. A few nights a week, we joined the Salvation Army in open-air evangelistic meetings in the nearby towns of Whitby, Brooklin, Pickering or Greenwood. It was inspiring to imitate a method used by Jesus himself. Several of us would fill up a big Model A Ford convertible, rumble seat and all, and head out to sing and preach. From this group of young Christians, God called four to be pastors and two to be missionaries in South America.

The schoolhouse in Ajax was eventually crowded to capacity with people of all ages coming to listen to the preaching of the gospel. A few weeks after becoming a Christian, I was assigned to teach a class of 9 to 12 year-old boys. Between 15 and 25 boys attended my Bible class each Sunday afternoon. It was a tremendous learning experience for me.

Around the same time, my friend, Tom Delaney, also felt God's call to ministry. He suggested we apply to Toronto Baptist Seminary. To my amazement, we were both accepted. I had only been saved about four months and was not yet baptized, because there was no baptistery in the schoolhouse where we worshipped. I had to wait several months until a baptismal service was organized at Calvary Baptist Church in Oshawa.

The Lord met all my financial needs. He provided me with part-time jobs as well as gifts from a number of generous people. My brother Lorne decided to drive a milk truck in addition to his responsibilities on the farm to help pay for my seminary education. He did this for a year before the Lord also called him into ministry, and he joined me at Toronto Baptist Seminary in 1944.

My mother considered it a great blessing to have three sons enter the ministry (my brother George became an officer in the Salvation Army). Out of seven boys, Lorne was the only one who had expressed interest in taking over the family farm. That hope was lost when he left for seminary, but my father enjoyed robust health and continued to run the farm until he was well into his eighties. He gradually sold off the 100 acres of land to a housing developer, but continued to live in the original farmhouse almost to the end of his days at the age of 107. My mother had passed away seven years earlier at the age of 91.

Seminary was the beginning of a completely new life. When I started studying to become a pastor, a worker in the kingdom of heaven, I had no idea where God would lead me. But God in his eternal plan sent me to a seminary where the faculty was deeply concerned for the spiritual needs of the province of Quebec.

2

A clear call to Quebec

"I know your works. See, I have set before you
an open door, and no one can shut it."
Revelation 3:8a

Toronto Baptist Seminary was a vital training ground for evangelical Baptist pastors. It had been founded by Christians who were seeking to resist the invasion of liberal theology in seminaries of the day. One of these individuals was Dr. T. T. Shields, who was President of the seminary and pastor of Jarvis Street Baptist Church. Dr. Shields was a big man with strong convictions. His patriotism, for instance, led him to close the seminary for several years during the Second World War so as to encourage as many men as possible to enlist.

I was one of 25 young students who attended the seminary when it reopened in the fall of 1943. When the war ended, the return of the veterans swelled enrolment to approximately 75.

As a new Christian, I was totally unaware of the needs of the mission fields of the world. However, the faculty at the seminary, notably Dr. W. S. Whitcombe, felt a special burden to train workers to reach the neglected province of Quebec. The spiritual needs of French Canadians were often presented by various speakers in our daily chapel services. So it was that we learned that the number of French evangelicals of any stripe or colour was extremely small in this province of over four million people. In response to their deep-seated concern for Quebec's spiritual needs, the seminary leaders required every student to study French.

In 1944, after my first year of seminary, I spent the summer in Geraldton, 870 miles northwest of Toronto. After a 20-hour train ride, I arrived in this isolated gold-mining town of 5,000 inhabitants where they still had wooden sidewalks and dirt roads. As the summer pastor, I lived in the back of the Baptist church on the edge of town from April to September.

It was a shock to be so far away from home for the first time, and I was terribly lonesome. My mother tried to ease my homesickness by sending small care packages from time to time. On one occasion, when I went to the post office to pick up my mail, the attendant disappeared into the back room and returned with an offensive smelling parcel held at arm's-length. My mother had sent me a dozen eggs which, of course, had broken in transit and gone bad!

After my second year of seminary, I had the opportunity to work in the northwestern region of Quebec, only 430 miles from Toronto. The small English Baptist church in Noranda was without a pastor, and I was invited to fill the position for the summer.

The twin cities of Rouyn-Noranda formed a bustling mining centre of 25,000 people. During the Depression and the war years, many Canadians and a significant proportion of immigrants had come to find employment in the region's copper and gold mines. Rouyn was predominantly a business district with a French-speaking majority. Noranda, on the other hand, was essentially a residential area constructed by Noranda Mines for its workers, most of whom spoke English.

My first summer in northwestern Quebec was a real eye-opener. For the first time in my life, I was immersed in a community where thousands of people did not speak English. With my rudimentary French skills, I began conversing with French Canadians and was shocked to learn that some of them had never heard of the New Testament. I also realized that millions of French-speaking people had little or no knowledge of the Word of God and the true message of the gospel. My burden for them began to grow.

Seminary days

During the winter months that followed, I concentrated on doing everything possible to learn French. Several other seminary students shared this passion, and we organized French discussion groups and evening meetings to practice the language. When we met in various homes in the evenings, we performed skits in French, re-enacting evangelism visits. These were quite funny and also profitable, as we exercised not only our language skills but our witnessing abilities as well. We had what we called "the French table" during the dinner hour at seminary, for anyone who wanted to speak only French. A 25-cent fine was charged for any word spoken in English. That was big money in those days.

Summer in Malartic

The following summer, I returned to northern Quebec. This time I worked in the town of Malartic, a half-hour drive from Rouyn-Noranda.

Malartic had the appearance of a frontier town because it had been rapidly built to meet the demands of a sudden influx of workers after gold was discovered there in the 1920s.

I worked under the supervision of Pastor Wilfrid Wellington, who was responsible for the Malartic church as well as the church in Val d'Or, a larger gold-mining town nearby. He placed me in charge of all the summer church activities in Malartic, including the construction of a modest church building.

Within days of my arrival, I was invited to participate in my first open-air meeting in Quebec. With some apprehension, I joined Edna and Wilfrid Wellington and a few other English Christians in front of the Beau Chêne Hotel in Malartic. The hotel was a popular place in town with a bowling alley and poolroom. Three or four long wooden steps in front of the building provided a natural amphitheatre.

Soon after our arrival, a crowd of people gathered to listen to our music and our message. We took turns speaking, interspersing our short messages with hymns. The sun went down, the city lights came on and still the crowd stayed.

When the meeting finally ended, a police car drove up and the chief of police announced that we were no longer permitted to preach in front of the hotel. I was surprised to hear this, because the meeting had proceeded in an orderly fashion, with no obstruction to traffic, and the assembled crowd seemed so anxious to hear us speak. The chief of police would not answer our questions, but insisted we go to the station for further discussion.

At the station, the chief explained that there were so many people listening to us on Saturday nights that the beer parlour, the pool hall and the bowling alley were empty. He was afraid the owner of these establishments was going to go bankrupt. We later went to see the owner of the Beau Chêne Hotel. He admitted that on Saturday nights business was almost down to zero during the meeting, but he did not mind at all because it gave him an opportunity to go outside and listen too.

Despite the owner's good will, the chief of police required us to meet the mayor and the city council to obtain permission to continue open-air meetings. Several English-speaking people from the church came with us to the council meeting. When the time came, the chief of police rose and explained that the Baptist meetings on Saturday nights were very annoying to the owner of the building and adversely affected his business. In turn, I countered that the owner had no objections to our meetings and was perfectly willing for us to continue.

Dead silence fell over the council room and we waited for the mayor to render his decision. Finally he told us that the city council had no authority to either grant us a permit, or to deny us permission to meet. It was not their department and they had no authority to stop us. We were elated! The meetings continued throughout the summer and were used mightily by God for the salvation of French Canadians.

On one occasion, Wilfrid Wellington gave a New Testament to a man in the crowd who had been deeply touched by our message. He became one of the first converts in the Malartic church. Years later his grandson, Arnold Boulianne, became a Baptist pastor.* Other key workers emerged from those early converts in the pioneer days of evangelism in Quebec. These are some of the *footprints* the Lord has allowed me to see during my lifetime.

A growing conviction

My summer of evangelism in Malartic increased my conviction that God wanted me to serve among French-speaking people after my graduation from seminary. During the final years of my seminary training, Yvon Hurtubise became my roommate. Yvon was French-speaking and had come to the Lord under the ministry of Pastor J. R. Boyd in the Sudbury area. Yvon was also preparing for full-time service to French Canadians, and our time together helped me to improve my fluency in French.

In many different ways, my experiences at seminary were a learning process. One of my goals was to become an effective preacher whom God could use to lead people to salvation. When I returned from my summer ministry in Quebec, I presented a report at our annual convention one day and spoke at the seminary chapel service the next day. Afterwards, I noticed a note addressed to me on the bulletin board from the dean of the Seminary, W. Gordon Brown. It read simply: "Heron - *please see the Dean in his office.*"

I was puzzled. I had no idea why Dean Brown wished to speak to me. I knocked on his office door and entered with some trepidation. He invited me to sit down and, without further ado, said, "Heron, if you continue to do what you are doing now, you might as well quit seminary." I was totally taken aback. What grave error I had committed? Dean Brown continued: "Do you know that when you spoke in the chapel service this morning for approximately ten minutes, you stroked the side of your nose 33 times. I know, because I counted. You spoke at the convention yesterday, and a woman approached me afterwards and asked, 'Why is it that your student, Murray Heron, strokes the side of his nose so often when he speaks?' "

The Dean pointed out that if I continued this distracting habit, it would

---

* Arnold married Keren Whitehead, who came to Quebec as a single missionary from Ontario. Sensing God's call to Quebec, Keren learned French and came to work in our area. They have ministered in several Fellowship Baptist churches, including the French church in Verdun where my brother Lorne pastored for 19 years.

ruin my ministry. Then he asked, "Why do you do this?" I explained that my favourite preacher occasionally stroked the side of his nose when he preached, and that I admired him so much that I had begun to mimic him. He warned me that if I tried to imitate someone else, I would invariably end up adopting his faults as well. This memorable meeting with the Dean, whom I feared and respected, definitely cured me of my nose stroking habit before it got out of hand.

Student antics

On occasion, we seminary students showed more zeal than wisdom. Some of us wanted to try open-air preaching in Toronto. We went down to the busy corner of Shuter and Yonge Streets, where there were crowds passing by. We tried to attract people's attention for a while, but the culture in Toronto is quite different from that of Quebec, and we soon realized that no one was going to stop and listen to our message.

In desperation, we devised a way to get people to listen. Carefully placing a Bible on top of our portable organ, we covered it with our coats. Then we shouted: "Ladies and gentlemen, we are very happy to tell you that we have the greatest living thing in captivity and in a few moments we will show it to you. Draw closer, draw closer! You are going to have an extraordinary experience tonight. You will see the greatest living thing in captivity."

The building behind us happened to be filled with young people that evening. In no time at all, they spilled out onto the sidewalk, creating an instant audience. We continued with our enticing words: "Draw closer! Please do not block the sidewalk. In a few moments, you will see the greatest living thing in captivity!" When the crowd was so large that we could barely move, we whipped off the coats. Then we held up the Bible and proclaimed, "*This* is the greatest living thing."

The crowd was not amused by this deceptive tactic. Within minutes, everyone was gone except the young people from the building behind, who had unwittingly locked themselves out in their eagerness to hear us. We had learned a valuable lesson in realizing that our method was not an honourable way to preach the gospel.

Direction for the future

With graduation approaching, I faced a major decision about my future. I was asked to pastor a church in east Toronto which, humanly speaking, offered ideal conditions. I could remain close to my family and friends, without struggling to learn a new language and adapting to a different culture. However, a number of compelling circumstances left me no doubt concerning God's will for my life.

I had learned to love the culture and character of the French-Canadian people. I enjoyed the French language and was becoming more and more adept at speaking and understanding it. It was obvious that there were people in Quebec who were open and hungry to hear the Word of God and it was exciting to talk to them about the Lord. In spite of this, I wanted a clearer calling, so I did something I have rarely done in my Christian life: I prayed for God to give me a definite sign. I asked him for two conversions in the place where he wanted me to minister.

The English Baptist church in Noranda, Quebec, was looking for a pastor, and they invited me to preach for a weekend as a potential candidate. At the end of my Sunday morning sermon, a boy came forward in response to the invitation to accept Christ as his Saviour.† While I was talking with him in the office at the close of the service, there was a knock on the door. Standing there was a second boy who also wanted to accept Christ.

Meanwhile the members of the Noranda church held a business meeting and voted unanimously for me to become their pastor. I was thrilled to see the Lord honour my simple faith by giving me this sign as added assurance that he really did want me in Quebec.

In retrospect, I see that the church in Noranda provided an ideal training ground for me in the work that God had called me to do. The church owned a lovely white building in the heart of the twin cities of Rouyn-Noranda, giving us a visible presence in the community. It was a stable, well-established congregation with a core of solid Christian families who had a burden for their unsaved neighbours and the untapped mission field on their doorstep. Moreover, the church was experienced in evangelism through open-air meetings in a nearby park, and through an English radio ministry.

When I graduated in May 1947, I was just 22 years old and I had been a Christian for less than four years. As I moved to Quebec, my intention and my burden was not only to pastor the English Baptist congregation in Noranda, but also to begin evangelism and church-planting among French Canadians as soon as possible. I began my ministry with great joy. I was well aware, however, of the challenges ahead: a different language, a different culture, and almost unbelievable obstacles.

---

† This boy was Lloyd Dalzell, who years later, became my brother-in-law when I married his sister, Georgia.

3

Responding to hungry hearts

"So shall My word be that goes forth from My mouth;
It shall not return to Me void,
But it shall accomplish what I please,
And it shall prosper *in the thing* for which I sent it."
Isaiah 55:11

In the spring of 1947, the Quebec political scene was dominated by the firmly entrenched Union National party led by the strong-willed Maurice Duplessis. He held office for over 18 years, first from 1936 to 1939 and then from 1944 until his death in 1959. Although seemingly popular throughout his long political career, historians and political scientists later agreed that the Duplessis years were a dark, repressive period. Quebec did not keep pace with the social and political developments in other provinces, particularly in education and public health.

Violent opposition to the gospel in Quebec was nothing new. I read a startling article in the *Toronto Daily Star* the night I took the train from Toronto to northern Quebec to start my ministry at Noranda Baptist Church. It related the graphic story of a group of Christians in the city of Shawinigan, in the heart of Quebec, who experienced a terrifying confrontation.

The reporter described how a thousand people broke into the building rented by the Christians for a Bible study. The mob tore up the Bibles and hymn books, overturned the piano and even flipped over the pastor's car in front of the building. I asked myself, "What kind of opposition will I face if I undertake an aggressive ministry among these people who for generations have not had the opportunity of hearing the true gospel?"

I was single during my first five years in Quebec. For the first three years, I boarded with a French couple, Laurent and Rhéa Larose, giving me excellent training in the French language and culture. For the next two years, I lived with the Barnharts, a bilingual Christian family.

The Christians of the English church shared my burden for the people around them. Together we wondered what God was going to do to build his church. I gave a series of messages concerning the way in which the Holy Spirit worked to advance the kingdom of God. As we studied this important subject, the whole congregation became deeply convicted that God would call a great number of French Canadians to be his children. As a church we studied the Book of Acts, in which we saw how the Spirit of God had moved to save thousands of people in the early days of Christianity. We were convinced that Quebec was not a more difficult mission field than Jerusalem, whose people had crucified Christ, or any of the other cities the apostles visited.

We also looked at the lives of men such as Jonathan Goforth, the missionary who went to China and saw multitudes come to Christ. In America, God had used individuals like Dwight L. Moody in the nineteenth century to touch great throngs of people. History also revealed that in eighteenth-century England, the entire nation was stirred by the preaching of the gospel by John Wesley and George Whitefield.

We concluded that what God had done in other areas of the world, in other generations, he was still able to do in our time, in Quebec. We were confident that it was in the eternal plan of God to do a great work in this province of Quebec.

We were encouraged by what we found written in the first chapter of the Old Testament book of Joshua. The province was like the great land of Canaan, flowing with milk and honey, a land that God promised to give to the people of Israel. Our experience in open-air meetings in Malartic showed us that people were spiritually hungry. Individual contacts also convinced us that French Canadians were ready to listen to God's message.

Seeking soul finds salvation

As a perfect illustration of this readiness, the story of Georges Dallaire stands out in my mind. Pastor J. R. Boyd, a fellow pastor from Sudbury, sponsored a French radio program to reach northwestern Quebec from the town of Kirkland Lake just across the Quebec-Ontario border. Occasionally some of us ministering in Quebec were asked to conduct follow-up visits to people who had requested Christian literature or a New Testament. Thus, Pastor Wellington and Les Barnhart, a deacon from the Noranda church, went to visit Mr. Dallaire who lived about 90 miles south of Noranda. Although this man was illiterate, he had been listening to the radio program and was intensely interested in the gospel. He had become so preoccupied with his salvation that he asked his wife to write to the radio station to request a copy of the Bible and a hymn book.

When Pastor Wellington and Les Barnhart arrived at Mr. Dallaire's isolated home in the country, he greeted these servants of the Lord with great joy. He told them how he had hired a taxi and travelled 90 miles to Rouyn-Noranda in search of someone to explain the message of the Bible to him in French. But his journey had proved unsuccessful. Anyone he talked to was either unfriendly or unable to help him, and he had returned home without the knowledge he sought.

Still, there was a burning desire in this poor farmer's heart, so once again he hired a taxi and this time went 60 miles across the Quebec-Ontario border into the town of New Liskeard. He thought that in Ontario someone would certainly point him to the way of salvation, since this was "the province of Protestants." However, because he was unable to communicate in English, no one could help him and he again returned home disappointed.

The arrival of Pastor Wellington and Les Barnhart was an answer from God. After several hours of conversation, they asked Mr. Dallaire if he wanted to give his life to Christ. He answered that he had been waiting for this moment for years. Following a prayer for salvation, Mr. Dallaire asked if they could sing a hymn together. To the delight and amazement of the two visitors, this man who had never been to a church service in his life, sang verse after verse of the beautiful hymn, "I found a Friend, oh, such a Friend, He loved me ere I knew him." His wife had read the words to him from the hymn book they had received in the mail, and he had memorized them while listening to the melody on the radio!

The next year I had the joy of baptizing him when he came to Rouyn-Noranda to participate in one of our services. As he left the church, he shared with me how much he had enjoyed our Sunday services and he hoped to return again the following year.

The conversion of Georges Dallaire touched us all deeply. It convinced us that there was a host of people like this country farmer who were desperately seeking peace and hope through salvation in Jesus Christ. But we knew that, similar to the biblical land of promise, there were walled cities, armies with chariots of iron and warring tribes opposed to the entrance of God's people into that land.

The Roman Catholic Church was the cornerstone of French Canadian society, exerting a pervasive influence on all facets of life. I clearly remember the day Théodule Lachance walked into my church office with all his earthly belongings in two suitcases. He was an older man who had been living in a seniors' home operated by nuns and was one of the early converts from Roman Catholicism. While reading the Bible one day, he saw the passage concerning vain repetitions in prayer, so the next morning he did not bring his rosary beads to breakfast as was the custom.

The sister in charge warned him that he had to bring his rosary the following day or else he would be asked to leave the home. His conviction was clear. He answered, "Why wait until tomorrow? I have no intention of bringing them. I will leave today."

The far-reaching influence of the Catholic Church continued well into the 1960s when Quebec experienced what is known as the "quiet revolution." With new political leaders at the helm, the province modernized education and other social institutions. Around the same time, the Roman Catholic Church went through changes brought about by the Second Vatican Council, which left many of its followers perplexed and disillusioned. Church attendance decreased dramatically throughout the 1960s and 1970s as Quebec's society left behind its religious past, entered the modern era and became increasingly secular.

On the front lines

We were so concerned and convicted about reaching the lost, that we regularly called our little church to special prayer. Prayer became the basis of our ministry to French Canadians. We met very early in the morning and sometimes we prayed all night. We established a daily prayer meeting where people could come and go as their schedule permitted. We became convinced that God would do far more than we could ask or think.

Our primary method of outreach to French Canadians was through open-air meetings. We reasoned that if the people did not come to the church, the church would go to the people. Rouyn-Noranda had already had several years of open-air meetings in English. A few seminary students who had done evangelistic work in the area during the previous summers had also conducted some of these meetings in French.

Filled with the certainty that it was God's will for us to continue this type of outreach, I ventured out into the streets of Rouyn just a few weeks after I began my ministry in northern Quebec.

4

Facing prison bars

"Whether it is right in the sight of God
to listen to you more than to God, you judge.
For we cannot but speak the things
which we have seen and heard."
Acts 4:19b,20

Our first street service in downtown Rouyn in early July 1947 is etched in my memory. Seven Christians from the church had joined me. We had chosen a wide street where there was little traffic, and plenty of space to hold a meeting without any obstruction to vehicles. At the same time, the location was close to the main street where throngs of people passed by on a Saturday or Sunday night. We had just begun our preaching and singing to a fine congregation of approximately 100 people when, to our great surprise, two police cars arrived with six officers. They immediately ordered us into the cruisers and took us to the police station.

The police detained us for approximately half an hour while the chief investigated our literature. He then told us he would not permit us to hold meetings in Rouyn anymore. We were sternly warned that if we persisted, our new home would be behind the iron bars he pointed to, only a few feet away.

This was startling and difficult news. Within a few days I went to see the mayor, but he adamantly refused to grant us permission to preach on the streets of Rouyn. He reiterated the chief's warning that they would not hesitate to arrest me and lay charges that could bring a penalty of two months in the local jail.

The following week, I learned that the police had stopped members of the Salvation Army on Sunday night, even though they had already been preaching on the streets of Rouyn for eight years. They later received permission to resume their street meetings, but the city continued to deny us the same privilege.

I wrote to Dr. Whitcombe at the seminary in Toronto, asking for his godly counsel. He answered immediately by telegram, advising me to see the best lawyer in town at the expense of the Canadian Protestant League. The League's purpose was to defend and protect Protestants from threats to their civil and religious liberties. At this time in Canadian history, the social and religious climate was very tense between Protestants and Roman Catholics with much suspicion and mistrust on both sides.

I consulted Max Garmaise, an experienced Rouyn lawyer, who was well aware of religious opposition in Quebec. After explaining the situation to him, I was told such high-handed action on the part of the authorities should be shouted from the housetops. Mr. Garmaise asked for a few days to study the case before giving me his legal advice on the best course of action.

Meanwhile we obtained the permission to preach in Noranda, a town with more Protestants. On Saturday evening, July 12, we went to the borderline between the two towns, stood on Noranda soil and preached to an assembled crowd on the Rouyn side. We used these tactics because we were convinced of the importance of reaching the French-speaking people of Rouyn, and we saw open-air work as our best opportunity to do so. I feared that if the Rouyn authorities succeeded in silencing us, preaching would soon be stopped in Malartic, Val d'Or, and perhaps every other town in Quebec that needed to be evangelized.

On Sunday night, after the evening service at the church, we held a meeting in the park by the lake in Noranda. A crowd of close to one hundred gathered to listen to our preaching and singing. Within a few days, Mr. Garmaise informed me of his professional opinion. He felt that under Canadian law the Rouyn authorities had no legal right to imprison us simply for preaching on a quiet Rouyn street. He called the city's municipal bylaw *ultra vires*, which means it went beyond the scope of legal power or authority, contravening the fundamental rights of all Canadians to freedom of speech and assembly. On those grounds, he was willing to defend our rights in court and was confident we could win our case. Therefore his legal advice was that we should continue our meetings, knowing full well we would be arrested. This would then enable us to contest the bylaw in court.

However, before fighting on that front, we were advised to make an official written request to the mayor and the chief of police. Mr. Garmaise wrote the letter and mailed it on Tuesday, July 22. The following Friday he called to say the mayor had refused us permission. I felt that too much of the summer had been wasted already and told the lawyer I was going to preach in Rouyn on Saturday night.

I was apprehensive, yet anxious to do God's will in this matter. It was one of the most important decisions of my life, a step that would shape my entire future ministry. On one hand, I had always been a law-abiding citizen and felt that it was essential for a Christian to obey the law. However, the Bible also taught clearly that the Lord is our supreme authority. If the laws of man stand in the way of accomplishing the will of God, we are to give him first place.

I was reminded of Daniel in the Old Testament, who continued to pray despite the laws of the land forbidding him to do so (Daniel 6). I will never forget the moment I came face to face with this awesome decision. I knelt in my room and told the Lord that I was willing to do whatever he wanted me to do even though it might mean spending the rest of my life in a Quebec prison. I resolved that whatever the cost, I would do his will.

On Saturday morning, July 26, I left my place of prayer and went to the mayor's office to see if there was any possibility that he would relent and let us preach. I told him I had tried to cooperate in every way possible, yet now I had no choice but to preach the gospel. I said we were planning a meeting that night.

He was very upset and immediately grabbed the phone to advise the chief of police of our intentions, but the line was busy. I told the mayor I had really nothing more to say and suggested that he could tell the chief of police that I would be on the street at eight o'clock. With these words I left the mayor's office.

I informed two missionaries, Alice Moore and Eileen Veals, who were working with us in the Noranda church, of what had just happened and asked them if they were ready to go to jail for the gospel. They were willing. The three of us met at the church that Saturday evening for a time of prayer before going out to preach. Now, 50 years later, I still vividly recall those solemn moments when we sought God's grace, telling him we were ready to go, but asking him to close the door definitely if it was not his will.

At first it seemed impossible to start our open-air meeting that evening at eight o'clock as planned because of a steady downpour. We thought perhaps God was closing the door, but after we committed everything to the Lord, we opened our eyes to see streams of bright sunlight shining through the church windows. It was time to go. As the Lord said to Joshua, "Arise, go over the Jordan."

Arrested in Rouyn

On that warm July night in Rouyn, we were arrested and taken to the prison. We spent less than an hour locked behind iron bars while charges were laid and bail was arranged. I had the joy of telling the men in my cell of the Saviour who died for their sins. They listened intently.

When Murray Heron and two missionaries, Alice Moore and Eileen Veals, were arrested in Rouyn on July 26, 1947, for open-air evangelism, it raised national awareness of the situation in Quebec.

That evening I went home and typed a letter to my mother: "We are rejoicing in the assurance that the Lord will never leave us nor forsake us. It is indeed a privilege to be counted worthy to suffer shame for His name. I remember how I said that the Lord was numbered with the transgressors. He poured out His soul unto death. Surely we can do a little to repay such a tremendous sacrifice....Don't worry about us up here, as nothing has happened contrary to the will of the Lord."

The Canadian Press carried the story of our arrest and every newspaper office in Canada received the news. Suddenly thousands of Christians across our nation became aware of our critical situation. In homes and in prayer meetings all over our land, people began to pray.

The Canadian Protestant League, deeply concerned by this religious freedom issue, was eager to help. Events unfolded swiftly. On the Thursday evening following our arrest, the League organized a special meeting at Jarvis Street Baptist Church in Toronto. Over a thousand people came to demonstrate their support. Alice Moore and I were present to tell our story. By the following week a full account of the evening was printed in a special edition of *The Gospel Witness and Protestant Advocate*, a publication edited by Dr. T. T. Shields, making even more people aware of the details of our situation.

After the Toronto meeting, I travelled back to Rouyn on the night train. Upon my return I had a letter on my desk from the mayor and chief of police of Rouyn, granting us permission to hold street meetings on Mondays, the quietest night of the week. We recognized this as a partial victory, as we had previously been refused any meetings, on any streets, on any night, but we could not be satisfied with this small concession. If we were to reach the thousands of French Canadians in the region, we needed the liberty to preach on the weekends when the streets teemed with needy souls.

Nevertheless we took advantage of this new permission the following Monday. We were a little timid wondering what the outcome of the evening would be, but it was an exceptionally good meeting as scores of people lined the sidewalk peacefully and others listened from balconies and open windows.

Regardless of our new authorization, we still needed to go to trial for the charges laid against us in July. The Canadian Protestant League retained a prominent Montreal lawyer, Harold Cotton, to defend us along with our lawyer from Rouyn. The trial was postponed for a number of weeks until our attorneys were available to represent us. Magistrate Felix Allard of Amos presided over our trial which lasted nearly three days, concluding on Wednesday, October 1, 1947. Our case received detailed coverage across

Canada and in parts of the United States. Even *Time Magazine* in New York gave a brief report of the trial.

Our lawyers did an excellent job of presenting the argument for our defense. The town argued that we were denied permission to preach in the street because of traffic concerns. But when Mr. Cotton cross-examined the mayor, it became evident, beyond all doubt, that we were stopped because of definite discrimination against us. The permit we had been granted after our arrest was valid only for Monday nights, whereas the Salvation Army had obtained permission to hold meetings any time or place in town, except Saturday night or pay night.

The press reported Harold Cotton's summary of the case based on the argument that the bylaw itself was *ultra vires*:

> This by-law is repugnant to the fundamental rights, liberties and freedoms of the town of Rouyn. Freedom to get together and discuss things in a peaceable manner is fundamental to our whole civilization. Without these fundamental rights we are behind an iron curtain.

Due to the publicity generated by the trial and the importance of his decision, Magistrate Allard wanted considerable time to review all the arguments of the case before pronouncing judgment. The judge's decision was scheduled for early November.

A new obstacle in our path

While the judge's decision was pending, the police continued their determined effort to oppose our preaching. At the end of October a new obstacle was placed in our path. The Noranda Church had been distributing the Word of God through door-to-door visitation for quite some time, but it now appeared that this freedom was also in jeopardy.

On October 30, 1947, Eileen Veals was visiting homes in Rouyn and giving out copies of the Gospel of John, when she was accosted by a priest who said she could no longer distribute this book. A few minutes later the police arrived and took her to the station. She was warned that she was transgressing the law and was threatened with arrest if she continued.

Eileen had given out close to 100 Gospels of John in two weeks. Most people had eagerly received the Word, and very few had refused a copy. We felt a deep conviction that God wanted us to continue offering the message of life through the printed page, and chose to continue this ministry despite the opposition of the city bylaw. Eileen bravely resumed visitation the very next day. I suspected that the previous day's warning was simply an attempt at intimidation and that the police would not dare attract the unwanted attention of the press by arresting a woman for distributing the Word of God. As expected, she was able to continue undisturbed.

Nonetheless, in an effort to be as cooperative as possible, we visited the mayor armed with a New Testament, a Gospel of John and a tract entitled *Four Things God Wants You to Know*. We explained that our only desire was to give people an opportunity to read the Scriptures for themselves.

He informed us that the city had adopted a bylaw that stated:

> Every person, institution, society or association whatsoever is forbidden to distribute to any person whatsoever and or in any place whatsoever or in any manner whatsoever pamphlets or leaflets or any literature under whatsoever form without previously having obtained a special permit from His Honor the Mayor or from the chief of police.

Furthermore, the mayor told us he was unwilling to grant us the freedom to give out our literature. Nevertheless, we submitted a written application requesting official permission.

Rouyn's bylaw was clearly a serious violation of the freedom of speech. This law essentially gave two men the control of what people could read. The editor of the local newspaper was indignant when he heard of this municipal rule. He commented, "This means the law is violated every time one of my newspaper boys sells a copy of my paper."

When November arrived, the date of our judgment was delayed until December and then it was postponed again until January. Undeterred by what appeared to be simple delay tactics, we held another open-air meeting on a mild evening, December 13, 1947. This time Miss Eileen Veals, Miss Mabel Bourne, Mr. Leslie Barnhart and I were arrested.

5

Treated like criminals

What then shall we say to these things?
If God *is* for us, who *can* be against us?
Yet in all these things we are more than conquerors
through Him who loved us.
Romans 8:31,37

On Monday, December 15, 1947, the press gave the following report:

> Mr. Heron, with Eileen Veals, 30, Mabel Bourne, 35, and Leslie
> Barnhart, proprietor of a large groceteria in Rouyn, were
> arrested Saturday night on charges of conducting a street
> meeting without a permit. All were kept in custody over the
> week-end and released this morning on bail.
>
> According to Mr. Heron…this time [they] received the full
> treatment usually reserved for criminals. On Sunday morning
> they were all aroused at 6:30 to be finger-printed and have their
> pictures taken.
>
> "A constable shouted at us to get up," said Miss Veals. "Later
> he shouted at us again and asked us if we were ready. We came
> out and they took our pictures and put convict numbers in
> front of us."

The cell in which she and Miss Bourne had to spend the night with four
girls who had been sentenced to Ville Marie Prison, was "terrible," said Miss
Veals. "I was practically ill on Sunday morning," she said. "There was only
space for four women there. I had to sleep on the floor on a straw mattress."

Miss Bourne said the cell was "disgraceful." "I am a registered nurse and
probably noted it particularly," she said. "There were no slip-covers on the
mattresses. We didn't know who had been sleeping on them before us. I

Newspaper headlines from 1947 and 1948 reveal the turbulence of these years for Murray Heron and other Baptists in Rouyn.

didn't sleep a wink. There was no ventilation and the air was foul."

On Sunday, the men held a service and sang hymns and prayed. The other men in the jail joined in. The girls were not permitted to take part, and their cell was too small for a service to be held there.

Bail of $25 each was paid by Mr. Barnhart when they appeared before Justice of the Peace J. H. Forget. The case was adjourned because Magistrate Felix Allard of Amos was not expected back in Rouyn until January, and his decision on our first trial was still pending. These were very dark and difficult days. We constantly sought the guidance of the Lord and prayed that he would give us freedom to preach.

We heard of a few church leaders who disapproved of our defying the municipal law. But for the most part, we had widespread support from churches across Canada. Some churches and groups cancelled their Bible studies to spend evenings in prayer on our behalf. Years later we still hear of families who prayed for us around their kitchen tables.

A number of my colleagues at the church wanted to hold another street meeting the weekend after our December arrest, but I felt that our goal was to preach the gospel, not to fight or irritate the authorities. We decided to wait for the official court decision before resuming street preaching.

Mr. Barnhart sought counsel from our Montreal lawyer, Mr. Cotton. He was advised that it was within our rights to sue the city, as the police had overstepped the limits in handling us like criminals for contravening a minor city bylaw. The goal of the lawsuit would not be to obtain monetary compensation but rather to have a bargaining tool to negotiate with the Rouyn authorities. Thus, a $5,000 lawsuit was filed in Mr. Barnhart's name against the city and the chief of police.

Fire destroys prison

The judge wasn't expected to render a decision on our July arrest until mid-February 1948, but without advance warning our attorney, Mr. Garmaise, called to say the magistrate was in town and ready to conclude our case on Tuesday, January 20. Mr. Garmaise also told me of a strange event that had happened on that very day. He described how a raging fire had swept through the prison, the police station and the city offices, destroying most of the building.

I went to look at the crumbled shell of the building and saw the cell where I had been detained reduced to ashes and twisted steel. The fire department was right next door to the prison and there was a competent staff of firefighters on duty with the most modern equipment, yet I marvelled that they had not been able to prevent the complete destruction of the edifice. Was God stretching out his arm to reveal his faithfulness to the preaching of the gospel?

The flames had not damaged the adjoining court area because it was protected by a fireproof wall. Although the odour of smoke permeated the premises, the judge found a usable room and gave his decision that afternoon.

Despite what we considered a strong defense and overwhelming evidence in our favour, the judge said he had no jurisdiction to rule on the *ultra vires* nature of the bylaw. Rather, his task was to determine whether we had violated the existing municipal bylaw. Thus, he declared us guilty and sentenced us to 30 days in prison or a comparable fine. After pronouncing our sentence the judge added that he hoped he would not have to preside at the trial arising from the December charges.

I was fined $25 and $45.10 in court costs. Alice Moore and Eileen Veals were also found guilty and each fined $5 and $42.90 in court costs. Although we had previously said we would rather go to jail than pay a fine, our lawyers advised us to pay the fine to facilitate our defense in contesting the injustice of further charges pending against us.

All these events brought tremendous publicity. I prepared a sermon entitled, "God Answers by Fire" and posted the title of my message outside the church door. I received a call from a *Toronto Daily Star* reporter who asked me if I was going to preach about the Rouyn fire. When I confirmed that this was my intention, he was eager to know what I was going to say. I gave him a brief summary of what the Word of God says about those who oppose God's servants.

Murray Heron pictured in front of his first pastorate, Noranda Baptist Church, in 1948.

I quoted the powerful words of Isaiah 54:17a: "No weapon formed against you shall prosper." I explained that it was not for me to say that God had burned down the jail, but it was evident that the building had been used as an instrument to stop the preaching of the gospel. The next day, my message and a picture of the demolished prison appeared in this Toronto daily, which was the largest English newspaper in Canada at the time.

About-face in Rouyn

Although the judge's decision appeared to be a severe blow against religious liberty, the extensive press coverage and the pressure of public opinion worked in our favour. We continued to pray that the Lord would cause the mayor of Rouyn to relent and grant us permission to hold meetings.

By the month of May, nothing had changed. Our December charges and Mr. Barnhart's lawsuit were still pending. I went to see the mayor to propose a solution to our stalemate before our case went to court. I boldly asked for the charges against us to be dropped and for permission to preach on Sunday nights. In exchange, we were prepared to drop our suit against the city. The mayor was willing to think it over.

We waited many days for a reply from the city and then finally on the very day we were to appear in court, I returned to the mayor's office and found that he had a letter for us on his desk. I was astonished by the mayor's complete change of attitude. The city granted us exactly the concessions we had sought: the charges against us were being completely removed from the books. The mayor would also write a letter to the chief of police giving us permission to preach and instructing the police to give us complete protection.

On May 20, 1948, *The Globe and Mail* of Toronto reported:

> Amicable settlement was announced today between the City of Rouyn and the four members of Noranda Baptist Church, including Rev. Murray Heron, in a long-standing dispute and court actions growing out of public meetings... [The] city has dropped the December charges against the four. A $5,000 action by Mr. Barnhart against the city and Chief Dussault also has been dropped. In addition, the city has agreed to permit public meetings by Mr. Heron on Sunday or Tuesday evenings on Noranda St., near Main St., in Rouyn.

I was overwhelmed by the Lord's gracious intervention. It was marvellous for the whole church to see the heavy clouds of opposition scatter and the bright light of victory shine through. When the warm weather arrived, we returned to the very spot where we had been arrested the previous summer and now preached with complete liberty. For the next 25 years, thousands of French Canadians heard God's message of salvation on this street corner in downtown Rouyn.

The end of our legal battle was only the beginning of frequent affronts, taunts and harassment from our detractors among the public. Some people resorted to all kinds of methods to interrupt our meetings and prevent others from hearing our message. Yet almost without exception, God provided a solution or used the incident to attract an even greater crowd.

There were also many calm open-air meetings over the years where spiritual seed was sown into the hearts of listeners. Typically, on Sunday nights during the summer months, the majority of the congregation accompanied me to a particular quiet street in Rouyn. Though there was little traffic on this street, we were close enough to Main Street to draw the attention of many people.

One evening when we began the meeting, a growing crowd gathered around us. Soon the entire area was filled with people and our audience was spilling over onto Main Street. We were always careful not to obstruct traffic in any way, but on this particular evening the group was getting so large that it was hampering the flow of vehicles.

We had to make a quick decision. On the one hand our goal was to give our message to as many people as possible, but on the other, we wanted to avoid problems with the authorities. There was no time to call a special meeting or consult anyone, so I simply moved out before the crowd and said to them, "If anyone wants to hear more of what we have to say, follow me." Then I turned and started to walk down the street away from the problem area. It was amazing to see that great host of people follow me. Soon we were some distance from the traffic and this large, attentive audience listened to the gospel as we sang and preached.

At the beginning of the meeting that evening, a man pushed forward through the large crowd to ask me some questions. I told him it was not convenient to answer him at that moment, but if he would wait to the end of the meeting I would be happy to spend time with him. Even after the long service this man emerged from the crowd once again with his spiritual questions.

Week after week during the summer it was a thrill for me to conduct street meetings for Quebeckers who were obviously eager to hear the gospel. Although we had taken a difficult stand that involved a great deal of sacrifice, the Lord granted us a joyous freedom to proclaim the gospel in the same place where the authorities once told us we would never preach again.

6

Over the air waves

For the word of God is living and powerful,
and sharper than any two-edged sword.
Hebrews 4:12a

Even before my arrival, the Noranda church had a 15-minute English
radio program every Sunday, and once a month the whole worship service
was broadcast. As our church became increasingly aware of the readiness
of our French-speaking neighbours to respond to the gospel, we felt it was
our duty before God to give them every possible opportunity to hear the
message of salvation. We prayed about starting a French radio ministry,
something that had never been done before in Quebec. Until then, the
only French evangelical radio programs heard in the province came from
border stations in Ontario.

When I suggested to some members of the church that we should seek
permission to use the powerful instrument of radio to spread the gospel,
many thought it could not be done. At the time, religious and social norms
were very rigid—anglophones were Protestant and francophones were
Catholic. This assumption permeated almost every layer of society. One
person told me I would just be wasting my time, as it was certain the radio
station would refuse us. Nevertheless, leaning on God's promise to give us
the souls of men for his glory, I undertook the application process in
September 1948.

On Saturday morning, September 11, I met with the station manager of
Radio Rouyn-Abitibi Limited. I was startled by his willingness to permit us
to have a program on his network of stations. When he asked me when I
would like to begin, I answered, "As soon as possible." So that very morning
we signed a one-year contract for weekly programs on Sunday mornings
from 10:15 to 10:30 A.M. at a cost of $8.50 per week. The first program
began the next day.

A typical radio program included a musical introduction, an offer of a New Testament, another hymn and a short sermon, followed by more music and an encouragement to write to us. A newsletter dated March 28, 1949, that we sent out to supporters and friends, called *The Baptist Broadcast*, indicates the effectiveness of the radio messages and the openness of our audience:

> We rejoice that the Gospel is now going out over the air in the French language from Radio Stations in Timmins, Kirkland Lake and Rouyn-Noranda. From the two counties adjoining Rouyn-Noranda alone, 1,080 have written requesting the Word of God. This great host of men and women represent 91 different towns, villages and communities.

Just one year later I wrote in this newsletter:

> It has been a joy to see the abundant fruits from this 15 minutes every Sunday morning. Most of our new converts have been contacted through this means. It is impossible for us to estimate the tremendous value of this program, as hundreds of people hear the Gospel in their native tongue, every week....[The radio station has] generously given us some free time in English as well. We broadcast our Sunday morning service once a month from the Church auditorium, without any charge.

Over the years, the programs evolved and by 1958 we had a half-hour of air time. Gradually we also had the opportunity to expand our range and broadcast from the four stations of Northern Radio in Rouyn, La Sarre, Val d'Or and Amos. This radio ministry continued for close to 30 years until we left the area in 1977.

The impossible happens

The reactions of the people who heard the broadcast were varied. The newsletter from the Noranda Church tells this story:

> A French Canadian Christian coming to Rouyn from the Montreal area said recently that he could hardly believe his ears when he turned on his radio one Sunday morning and to his amazement listened to the local station broadcasting an evangelistic program in the French language. Familiar with missionary

work in Quebec province, he stated that as far as he knew, it was the only program preaching the Gospel in the French language anywhere within the borders of the province. We never cease to thank God for this great open door, on four stations, reaching thousands of lost souls with the Good News of salvation.

Another excerpt from *The Baptist Broadcast* reports:

> From different parts of northwest Quebec people write from time to time telling us that they listen to our weekly broadcasts. This week we were overjoyed to receive a letter from a man who has been an ardent radio listener for many months telling us that while listening to our broadcast he came to the assurance of his salvation in the Lord Jesus. On different occasions he has written asking questions concerning the way of life. A few weeks ago he made the trip to town just to talk about the Bible. He now sends this wonderful news. 'Dear Pastor, I cannot express all the joy and happiness that I have experienced, for on the 13th of March your words gave me the assurance that I have found what I need for the salvation of my soul. I ask myself again today what divine power urged me to see you. I am happy and thank our Lord Jesus Christ for having thus inspired me.'

Many of the letters that we received greatly encouraged us to press on in this work. For instance, here is a letter from a man living a hundred miles away:

> Having heard you several times on the radio let me take this opportunity to write you because I notice that there are good people outside the Catholic religion. I have been farming here for ten years and every one here is against me simply because I am not Catholic. I am 52 years old with 17 children living. I have been reading the New Testament for a number of years.

On the other hand, this letter from a very devout Roman Catholic is quite revealing about some of the beliefs of our listeners:

> Reverend Pastor, I am praying you would give your heart to Jesus by the very Holy Virgin Mary, his mother. Since God has seen fit to choose a mother for the redemption of the world it is because He considered her worthy. When Jesus died the last

drop of his blood fell into the heart of his mother, she fainted, her sacrifice was complete. So you might better understand I am sending you a catechism of Christian doctrine. When you are sufficiently enlightened, go and find a priest, he will receive you with open arms. I am sending you a miraculous medal, wear it, it will bring you happiness.

Strong opposition turns to conversions

Due to this radio ministry, I had an opportunity to visit a Mr. Vezina. The first time I visited him, his two teenage daughters were very displeased. When they arrived home from school and realized their father was talking to the radio preacher, they became visibly upset, stomped across the living room, and disappeared into their room slamming the door behind them.

Despite this stormy start, the Lord later touched the hearts of the two daughters, Denise and Huguette. Both accepted the Lord and came to church with their father. Years later Huguette's daughter, Linda, became the wife of Toe-Blake Roy who now pastors a French Baptist church in Lachute, Quebec.

Preaching the good news through radio allowed us to reach the hearts of many people with God's Word. It also proved to us that the Lord really did intend to give us every place the sole of our foot should tread upon.

7

More workers in the harvest

"Behold, I will make you into a
new threshing sledge with sharp teeth;
You shall thresh the mountains and beat *them* small,
And make the hills like chaff."
Isaiah 41:15

The Lord abundantly rewarded the concern and efforts of our congregation for lost souls. As adults and young people in the Noranda church became living testimonies for Jesus Christ, we witnessed a significant response to the gospel among both francophones and anglophones.

The busy Sunday schedule began in the morning at the radio station. Then the church building became a hive of activity with English Sunday school followed by a worship service. Although the English were in the minority in the city, more and more people were coming to Christ. The Sunday school grew and a large number of young people attended the services and special meetings.

Sunday afternoons, the chapel housed a French Bible school followed by a meeting for the growing francophone congregation. It was absolutely thrilling to see French Canadians coming to these services, hearing the gospel for the first time and finding Christ as their Saviour.

These were exciting times in the life of the church. The two language groups met separately, but joined together every month for the Lord's supper and for special occasions such as baptismal services, the reception of new members and church business meetings.

Businessman enters the ministry

A year after Mr. Les Barnhart willingly faced opposition for his faith, the Lord called him into full-time ministry. Mr. Barnhart was a member of our church and a prosperous businessman as the owner of Rouyn's largest grocery store.

I vividly recall sitting with Les and his wife, Jo, in their comfortable home as he told me of his decision to sell his business. He had a burden to reach the lost and in particular felt a call to minister to French-speaking people in the region. In December 1948, I asked Les to share his testimony from the pulpit of the church and tell of his call to ministry. He recounted how he had left his hometown of Fort Erie, Ontario, during the Depression to pursue work in northern Ontario when he was 18 years old. He worked in a grocery store and also as a door-to-door salesman of Rawleigh Products and Fuller Brushes. One night in January 1933, a friend told him about salvation in Christ. By 1:30 in the morning, he was convinced of his lost condition and accepted Jesus Christ as his Lord and Saviour.

His life was transformed. Worldly pleasures and companions were soon abandoned in favour of his new life. However, he found his long-standing smoking habit impossible to break. Since he thought smoking was a bad testimony for a Christian and found himself unable to give it up, he reasoned that it was not God's will for him to become a preacher.

Instead, he invested in the grocery business and devoted much of his spare time to Sunday school and church work. He moved to Rouyn in 1937 to become a grocery store manager and four years later acquired his own store. God blessed his business and it prospered.

Les participated in street meetings with the Noranda Church but felt uncomfortable about his smoking habit and decided he had to give up one or the other. So he prayed for God's intervention and God graciously delivered him from the desire for tobacco. It was then that he sensed God's call to vocational ministry.

The *Rouyn-Noranda Press* printed a full account of Les' presentation at the church, concluding with this quote:

> Perhaps there is someone that would think that I have done some great thing, but I would like to assure you that I have done nothing. My only aim in selling my business and in doing what I have with the proceeds, is that I may tell the unsearchable riches of Christ without being hampered and tied down with the petty things of this world.

A few months later at our annual business meeting, the church voted unanimously to appoint Les as our full-time missionary to French Canadians with the intention that he would hold meetings and visit contacts throughout the whole area. The Barnharts continued to live in

Noranda and carried out their ministry under the guidance of the Noranda church for a number of years. Their work was financed from the profits of the sale of their business.

The addition of a committed man like Les to the French work in northern Quebec was a great encouragement to me, and a real answer to our prayers to send more workers into God's harvest.

Turbulent days in La Sarre

Les and Jo felt a special burden for the area around the town of La Sarre, a farming district known as the great clay belt, 55 miles north of Rouyn-Noranda. Already the Lord had saved a number of French Canadians in that area and a fine group of believers had formed a zealous church ready to witness for Christ. They had even constructed a small building east of the town.

In the summer of 1950, Les led an aggressive campaign in La Sarre. For the first time, open-air meetings were held in the town. Young men and women from both Toronto Baptist Seminary and Central Baptist Seminary came to join forces with the church over the summer months for this evangelistic effort.

As in Rouyn-Noranda and later other areas of Quebec, this thrust met with bitter hostility. The eruption of severe conflicts between town authorities and Baptist missionaries once again became the subject of press coverage, and reporters were dispatched to the area.

On Saturday, July 22, 1950, I received a visit from two Toronto reporters. They had heard of our work and wondered if they should go to La Sarre or Val d'Or where there was also an ongoing evangelistic effort and harsh opposition. I told them the choice was theirs as open-air activities were taking place in both communities. They chose La Sarre.

Later that same night, I was at the church when the two reporters burst into my office, very excited and agitated. They had observed the events in La Sarre from a rented hotel room overlooking the street meeting. From this vantage point, they witnessed a mob scene they would never have believed had they not seen it with their own eyes.

On Monday morning, Toronto's big daily newspaper, the *Evening Telegram*, printed a front-page story of the Saturday night events by reporter Don Delaplante. The headline read: "Egg, Kick, Jail Baptists as Quebec Police Look On." He wrote:

> Five Baptist evangelists were showered with eggs, potatoes and rubbish, beaten and finally jailed in a mob scene involving 250 residents of this Northwest Quebec village Saturday night.

Today the five were awaiting trial on charges of illegal assembly.

The Baptists, victims of the riot—although seemingly willing victims—were charged with creating it when they would not obey the police orders to halt their meeting.

Football charges

Even as police talked to them, the Baptist men were hurled about by jolting football-style charges from town hooligans who struck them with their shoulders and drove fists into their bodies. The Baptists would be driven 12 and 15 feet back into the mob, then strive to get back to the questioning police. They were slapped, kicked and yanked about by their ties.

Women of the group were jostled and struck with potatoes and other flying debris, but the vigorous bodily charges were restricted to the men. A laughing mob followed the Baptists as they were conducted to jail by Constable Edward Cloutier. As the mob continued to jeer through the jail windows the police chief set a guard of firemen over the prisoners. The Baptists replied by singing hymns as they waited.

Barnhart, Boillat, Rossignol and Cloutier each preached in turn to the firemen and spectators at the windows. Their efforts were met with hostile frowns and jeers.

This was the third attack upon the Baptists in La Sarre in the past three weeks. Last Saturday, the town fire department rushed up with its pumping unit and turned the fire hose upon the group. On July 8, the group's first meeting was broken up by a mob.

A stocky, fair-haired man who appeared to be a leader caught Boillat unawares as the Baptists stood face to face in conversation with Chief Carpentier. Boillat's head snapped back and his mouth fell open and he went to his knees.

The legs of another Baptist were grabbed from the rear and his feet yanked from under him. One man crouched behind Carr on hands and knees and another pushed him over.

One of the attackers appeared to be partly berserk or drunk. He charged about wildly screaming.

Eggs flew and all of the men were struck. Four struck Carr and three hit Boillat. One spattered from Boillat's head onto the tunic of the policeman.

A crowd of shouting youths closed in on them. A tall youth wearing a white sweatshirt pretended to lead their singing. His clownish antics drew laughter and people who had been waiting at their cars, moved across the street.

A small man wearing a peaked cap drove a new blue car around the corner, its horn screeching. He drove directly to the group and his bumper touched the men's legs. They would not move and he jumped out, shouting angrily. More angry shouts intermingled with the laughing taunts. The crowd proved to be of two moods, one deadly hostile, the other scornful.

Dust and refuse from the road was tossed into the air, it drifted down upon the singers, falling upon the women's hats and their hymnbooks. Potato chips were procured from a lunchroom and a shower of them was directed at the group.

One youth obtained a quantity of hamburger buns, chewed them, then threw the product at the singers.

Drown out hymns

A loud speaker was brought up on a car bearing the sign "Lapierre's Radio Service." Jazz music blared out at maximum volume. The hymns of the singers were unheard in the din. Debris continued to shower upon them from every side. More than 200 persons were jammed about them when Chief of Police Charpentier arrived.

A Quebec provincial policeman appeared at the intersection, directing traffic. He stayed on the road and did not go near the disturbance.

Suddenly the loud speaker began to play "Ave Maria." As the Catholic hymn poured forth, a peculiarly dangerous tension grasped the crowd. But the next record reverted to jazz which was played thereafter.

A group of powerful men began to use what appeared to be organized tactics to smash the group. They charged in football fashion, separating them from the women. They rushed from unexpected angles, hitting the men with bone-jolting force.

Murray Heron, pastor of Noranda Baptist Church and senior Baptist churchman in Northwest Quebec, claimed that the group had done nothing whatever to incite attack. He said the Baptists rigorously avoided references to the Catholic Church in their services and sermons in Northwest Quebec. "The imprisonment of these men is a great injustice," he stated.

This was an extremely dark hour. The police released the women of the group and one man, but five key workers were arrested and taken to the jail in Amos. The men, Leslie Barnhart, Maurice Boillat (a Professor at Central Baptist Seminary, Toronto), Lloyd Carr (a seminary student),

Egg, Kick, Jail Baptists As Que. Police Look On

CHARGE 5 EVANGELISTS WITH CREATING RIOT

By DON DELAPLANTE

La Sarre, Que., July 24—Five Baptist evangelists were showered with eggs, potatoes and rubbish, beaten and finally jailed, in a mob scene involving 250 residents of this northwest Quebec village Saturday night. Today the five were awaiting trial on charges of illegal assembly.

The Baptists, victims of the riot—although seemingly willing victims—were charged with creating it when they would not obey police orders to halt their meeting, even as police questioned them, their beating by town residents continued, without police interference as far as could be seen.

Jailed under section 87 of the Criminal Code were Leslie H. Barnhart, 37, pastor of the Bonn___ velle Baptist Church, four r___ of La Sarre; Maurice B___ ___rofessor of Fre___ ___ptist Seminary ___ Lloyd C___

the prisoners. The Baptists replied by singing hymns as they waited. Barnhart, Boillat, Rosignol and Clouthier each preached in turn to the firemen and the spectators at the windows. Their efforts were met with hostile frowns and jeers.

This was the third attack upon the Baptists in La Sarre in the past three weeks. Last Saturday, the town fire department rushed up with its pumping unit and turned the fire hose upon the group. On July 8 the group's first meeting was broken up by a mob.

A front page story in the Monday edition of Toronto's Evening Telegram *outlines the dark events of Saturday, July 22, 1950.*

Five key workers (Leslie Barnhart, Maurice Boillat, Lloyd Carr, Alphonse Cloutier and Noël Rossignol) were arrested in La Sarre and taken to the jail in Amos.

Alphonse Cloutier and Noël Rossignol (French believers from La Sarre), were all charged under the Criminal Code with holding an illegal gathering with the intention of disturbing the peace, a charge that could bring a sentence of up to five years of imprisonment.

The La Sarre authorities seemed convinced that our ministry was now overthrown and that they were permanently rid of the Baptists. Yet, we were equally certain of the Lord's promise that he would give us the land for his glory.

8

Opposition in La Sarre

"He delivered me from my strong enemy,
From those who hated me...
the Lord was my support.
He also brought me out into a broad place;
He delivered me because He delighted in me."
2 Samuel 22:18-20

Media reports of the weekend events in La Sarre brought a storm of protests against the town authorities. By Friday of the same week, July 28, 1950, the headlines of the *Rouyn-Noranda Press* proclaimed:

> *La Sarre Council Asks Provincial Police Aid*
> *—Mayor Is Bedridden After Baptist Brawl*
> The mayor was unconscious for 24 hours and still is too sick to receive visitors....Mayor Martel sustained an attack of angina pectoris after receiving many telegrams of protest from various parts of Quebec and Ontario regarding the treatment of the small group of Baptists who, Saturday evening, were buffeted by an angry crowd of at least 300 people on La Sarre's main street.

On August 3, 1950, the *Toronto Daily Star* published further developments:

> *La Sarre Mayor Dies, Blame Worry Of Baptist Incident*
> F. X. Martel, first mayor of the town of La Sarre, seized with a heart attack last week, died at his home here today.
> Mr. Martel suffered a seizure after having received a number of telegrams and other messages from different points in Ontario and Quebec denouncing treatment of Baptist church

LASARRE MAYOR DIES, BLAME WORRY OF BAPTIST INCIDENT

Special to The Star

LaSarre, Que., Aug 3—F. X. Martel, first mayor of the town of LaSarre, seized with a heart attack last week, died at his home here today.

Mr. Martel suffered a seizure after having received a number of telegrams and other messages from different points in Ontario and Quebec denouncing the treatment of Baptist church members near LaSarre, who had been the butt of much abuse as they attempted to hold an open-air meeting two Saturdays ago.

From the time he suffered the attack which most people believed was brought on by worry over the Baptist incident in which he had taken a leading part, little hope was held for his recovery.

Mr. Martel became the first mayor of LaSarre when it was incorporated as a town in September, 1949.

Surviving are his wife and 10 children. Funeral services are expected to take place Monday morning at the LaSarre Roman Catholic church.

Toronto Daily Star report of the death of the mayor of La Sarre, F. X. Martel. He suffered a heart attack after receiving telegrams and messages denouncing his treatment of the Baptists in La Sarre.

members near La Sarre, who had been the butt of much abuse as they attempted to hold an open-air meeting two Saturdays ago.

From the time he suffered the attack which most people believe was brought on by worry over the Baptist incident in which he had taken a leading part, little hope was held for his recovery.

A few days later the town council of La Sarre phoned our lawyer in Rouyn to arrange an urgent meeting. They hired a taxi and the entire town council travelled 55 miles to meet us at our lawyer's office.

We were taken aback by what we heard. They deeply regretted the arrests and shoddy treatment our men had received in the past weeks. They wanted the prisoners released immediately and were withdrawing all charges against them. In addition, they granted us permission to preach and promised police protection to prevent further ill treatment from the public in La Sarre.

We praised God for this sudden reversal. By the following Saturday night, the arrested preachers were back in La Sarre. Yet it soon became evident that there was still great animosity in this town.

On August 21, *The Toronto Telegram* printed a detailed account of another conflict in La Sarre under the headline: "Mob Baptist Group Hurl Firecrackers as PC Stands By."

> A Baptist revival meeting was violently broken up by a mob of youths in this northwestern Quebec lumbering town on Saturday night....
>
> Their voices lifted in a hymn and the youths started to dance around them, waving their hands and screaming abuse. The evangelists finished their hymn and Mr. Barnhart started to preach. The crowd had swollen to nearly 200 people, with the violent elements jostling the Baptists and elderly persons standing on the sidewalks, laughing and jeering.
>
> Suddenly there was a splutter of red flame and firecrackers began to explode around the Baptists' feet. Then the crowd started to hurl the crackers straight at Mr. Barnhart. They exploded in his face and bounced off his clothes.
>
> *Destroy Hymn Book*
>
> The blue haze from the fireworks that were cracking like machine-guns covered the crowd. Suddenly Mr. Barnhart's hymnbook was snatched from his hand and sent hurtling over the crowd where it was trampled in the dirt.
>
> A gang of youths charged the Baptist minister and sent him staggering. More firecrackers blazed red in the dusk. The crowd yelled and hooted with delight as a half-drunk lumberjack grabbed the small preacher by the shirt front and yelled abuse into his face.
>
> In desperation Mr. Barnhart called off the meeting and tried to get back to his car through the jostling crowd. Youths seized the bumpers of the car and rocked it from side to side and up and down. Every time he tried to back out they pushed the car against the curb.
>
> Mrs. Barnhart got out and appealed to the crowd to let them go, but she was greeted with screams and abuse. Then someone let the air out of one of the back tires.
>
> *Painful Injury*
>
> Mr. Barnhart got out to try and fix it and firecrackers were thrown into his face as he bent over the wheel. The jack was kicked away from under the car and the pastor's hand was crushed between the tire and the fender. Although the town council of La

Sarre promised the evangelists protection, the town's six-foot constable, Edward Carpentier, did not appear until nearly ten o'clock, when the preacher was still trying to get away.

Mr. Barnhart put his head inside the trunk of the car to get at some tools and the catch was knocked free so that the trunk cover crashed down on the back of his head.

White and shaken, the Baptist minister held his head for a moment while the crowd roared with laughter. The policeman stood by Mr. Barnhart's side and laughed with the crowd.

At about 10:30 p.m. Mr. Barnhart gave up trying to fix the tire, and his wife managed to get to a taxi stand. The minister worked his way through the crowd and half fell, half crawled into the cab.

As this reporter left town, a rock crashed against the side of the truck.

"Go back to Ontario!" someone shouted. "You won't put our pictures in the papers."

Yet, the Lord stood by his people and strengthened their faith in the midst of this trial.

Noisy meeting in Macamic

During the early 1950s, the work in La Sarre and surrounding district continued to be an outreach ministry of Noranda Baptist Church and as the pastor, I endeavoured to help in any way I could. We were grateful for students from both Toronto Baptist Seminary and Central Baptist Seminary who came as summer workers and others the Lord brought in to lend a hand. Helen Hall of Hamilton, the daughter of Rev. Morley Hall, a Baptist minister, first came to our region as a teenager. She assisted with door to door literature distribution and participated in street meetings.

I distinctly remember an open-air meeting held in the town of Macamic, situated about 20 miles east of La Sarre. It was a warm Tuesday night in the middle of the summer. We had spent the day visiting homes in the area and had planned an evangelistic meeting in the town for the evening. After supper we positioned ourselves in front of the local hotel, but few pedestrians paid any attention to us. We soon realized that most of the townspeople were at a ball game down the street.

Suddenly a car parked beside us and the driver began to blow his horn unceasingly. A few moments later, another car parked two or three feet away on the other side of us and did the same. The noise was deafening. It was impossible to hear the singing or preaching, but this was the Lord's undertaking because this steady screaming of car horns distracted the public from the ball game and drew a huge crowd to our meeting. Nevertheless it was still impossible to make ourselves heard over the din.

After some time, one of the drivers left, only to return a few moments later driving an enormous tractor. He now parked his huge machine in his previous parking spot, ceremoniously removed the muffler and turned up the engine. The man then left the tractor running while he went into a nearby beer parlor.

The gathered crowd wanted to hear what we had to say, so someone climbed up onto the tractor and turned off the engine. A blessed silence descended upon us as the sun was setting over Macamic. It was so quiet I turned and asked Helen Hall to sing a solo. She sang a hymn in French with words similar to the familiar English hymn of Isaac Watts: "When I survey the wondrous cross on which the Prince of Glory died, My richest gain I count but loss and pour contempt on all my pride."

The crowd listened attentively to the singing and then the preaching. We continued with more singing and more preaching during the long twilight hours of this northern summer evening until the city's lights came on. Finally we stopped when we had no more voice to preach or sing.

When we returned to our car that was parked a short distance from the meeting, we noticed two flat tires and upon closer inspection saw that the valves had been removed from the tubes. Someone had also pounded a piece of shovel handle up the exhaust pipe. The Lord had prepared a solution ahead of time as we had spare valves and pumped up the tires with little difficulty. I struggled with the shovel handle, but then a group of strong young men came by and when they saw my predicament, they helped me out.

We were soon on our way home, rejoicing because God had once more given us the opportunity of preaching his Word to French Canadians. As we drove back to the church in La Sarre, we were a carload of happy and thankful Christians, singing great hymns of victory.

Many months later, I met a couple in the La Sarre Church who had heard the gospel for the first time at that eventful meeting in Macamic. They were now saved, baptized and members of the church.

Almost into the river at La Reine

On another occasion we went to the town of La Reine, a quiet community, 20 miles west of La Sarre. We began an open-air meeting in the heart of the town and discovered once again that there was a ball game going on, but before long the spectators from the ballpark came to listen to us.

We were thrilled to have such a sizeable audience. Soon, however, we spotted troublemakers in the crowd. They began to throw a volley of lighted firecrackers at us while we preached. Firecrackers exploded all around us. Although some landed on my head and shoulders and on my Bible, not one of these exploded, yet every firecracker landing on the ground did. Despite the adverse conditions, car horns blowing, people shouting, and firecrackers exploding, we were able to share our message with a considerable number of people.

At the close of the service we made our way to our car but it was impossible to drive away as a great throng surrounded us. Some young men took hold of the vehicle and rocked it back and forth, up and down, and sideways. When we tried to go forward, they pushed the car backward, making the wheels spin and dig into the sandy surface. After many attempts, we were finally able to move the car through the crowd and head for home.

When we had driven a short distance, a carload of men passed us at great speed. A little farther down the road we came to a construction area where a temporary bridge without guardrails spanned a high ravine. When we drove onto this narrow link, we saw the car that had passed us earlier blocking the other end of the bridge. The occupants piled out of the car and walked toward our vehicle with the intention, undoubtedly, of rolling our car over into the creek far below.

Just seconds before they were able to lay hands on our car, another vehicle came up behind us. The driver was infuriated. He got out and shouted to the driver of the other car to free up the road. We recognized this man from the meeting earlier that evening. He had listened intently and had been irritated by the crowd's hostility.

It was a tremendous encouragement to us and in our eyes a definite sign of God's intervention for this man to arrive just in the nick of time to deliver us from certain danger. This was only one of many occasions when we saw the Lord protect us from individuals who were determined to prevent us from preaching.

Priest burns our mail

In the early 1950s, we learned that some of the mail we sent out was not always being delivered into the right hands. The post office served as the spiritual lifeline for hundreds of families scattered in far-flung areas where there was no church, or who were too far away for us to visit on a regular basis.

I met with some of our workers to discuss the mail situation. None of us knew what steps to take to correct this problem. We prayed and asked the Lord to intervene.

In 1951, a storm of protest swept across Canada when it was revealed that Father Alfred Roy, a Roman Catholic priest in St-Germain, had been burning Baptist mail for about three years.

God's answer was not long in coming. Shortly after our meeting, Les Barnhart visited the post office in the village of St-Germain, near Noranda, where people had informed us they were not receiving our literature. The clerk in the post office readily admitted that she never distributed any mail coming from the Baptists, but had "special orders" from the parish priest to give it to him.

A few days later, I met the editor of the local paper while having lunch at a Noranda restaurant. He was familiar with our activities and inquired if we were experiencing any further difficulties. I told him of our problem with the St-Germain post office and confided that we feared this practice might be widespread in the area.

The editor was outraged. He decided to investigate this country parish and speak to the priest personally to verify these claims. The editor was a faithful Roman Catholic, but said he could not tolerate anyone violating the privacy of a Canadian citizen by tampering with his mail.

A few days later, the wires of the Canadian Press carried the news that a Quebec priest admitted unashamedly that he regularly destroyed Baptist mail. On August 4, 1951, *The Telegram* reported: "Father Roy told a reporter the mail in question gave the people 'wrong ideas' and that he had been burning it for about three years. Of the Baptists he said: 'In La Sarre they had firemen and hoses to fight them. Here we haven't, so we use the weapons we can.' "

Another storm of protest swept across our country and Canada's Postmaster General sent in representatives to investigate. In a statement to the press, the Postmaster General said his department would do everything in their power to prevent a repetition of this incident.

The St-Germain postmaster resigned and charges were laid against the priest and the 16-year-old mail clerk involved. At their trial in September 1951, both pleaded guilty to tampering with the mail. Their lawyer asked the court to be lenient, arguing that Father Roy had no criminal intentions but acted to protect his parish from what he believed were "Communistic" attacks on the Roman Catholic Church. The clerk received a suspended sentence and the priest was sentenced to a $100 fine or one-month in jail. He paid the fine.

A number of editorials criticized the judge for giving such light sentences and accused the justice system of using a double standard for Catholics and Protestants. Yet we were satisfied that the Lord had answered our prayers swiftly, and we received no further complaint of our mail not being received. Once again as we trusted the Lord, we saw him crumble the walls of opposition.

9

Victory in Val d'Or

"For I, the Lord your God, will hold your right hand,
Saying to you, 'Fear not, I will help you.' "
Isaiah 41:13

Although I had my hands full with a growing church in Noranda and out-reach in the La Sarre area, I occasionally helped out my brother, Lorne, who had been in ministry in Val d'Or since 1948. Val d'Or was a large, gold-mining centre 65 miles east of Noranda. There too, the small English congregation felt a need to preach in the open air to reach French Canadians with the gospel.

Lorne encountered problems with the Val d'Or authorities for preaching on the street as early as 1949. A newsletter, dated Saturday, August 27, 1949, recounts that Lorne was transferred from the Val d'Or jail to the district prison in Amos to serve his time. Four others were also sentenced: Mr. and Mrs. Yvon Hurtubise to 30 days each, Mr. Malcolm Purcell to 13 days, and Miss Eileen Veals to 10 days behind bars for participating in an open-air meeting in Val d'Or. The judge had likened them to Nazis, "forcing people to hear what they do not want to hear."

Our newsletter, *The Baptist Broadcast*, clearly states the position of the missionaries:

> Because there is no violation of any law and because the Lord's servants are thus being abused solely because of the message of the Gospel, more open-air meetings are being planned. We can do no other. Can we allow ungodly men to thus trample under-foot the glorious message of salvation?
>
> Our ranks now have been seriously depleted. We are in urgent need of men and women who count not their lives dear for the Gospel's sake. The Word says: "Ye have not yet resisted

unto blood, striving against sin." "I beseech ye therefore
brethren by the mercies of God that ye present your bodies a
living sacrifice..." Will you say with Paul, "for I am ready not
to be bound only, but also to die at Jerusalem for the name of
the Lord Jesus."?

Many men and women answered this appeal and stepped out in faith to
face the opposition in Val d'Or. There were no funds to cover judicial
expenses in Val d'Or, so those involved stood in their own defense, and in
every case the court found them guilty and sentenced them to a fine or to
jail. To make a firm stand, all chose to serve time in jail.

Our church newsletters of the time give brief glimpses of prison life.
During September and October 1949, Rev. Wilfrid Wellington and Les
Barnhart were incarcerated in the district prison in Amos, where they
continued to evangelize. The newsletter tells of the conversion of a fellow
prisoner: "...it will be very difficult for him if he makes a bold stand in the
prison. According to the rules, the prisoners are obliged to attend Mass on
Sunday morning, or spend three days on bread and water, chained to their
bed in a private cell. Our missionaries were at first told that they must
attend, but later the official permitted them to remain behind without
punishment. Undoubtedly their new convert will not escape as easily."

Upon release from jail, Rev. Wellington and Les Barnhart spoke happily
of God's divine protection and sustaining grace during their days of confinement. The Lord had given them a unique prison ministry: 12 prisoners
and one guard had requested New Testaments.

Ongoing battle

The following summer, 1950, while the work in La Sarre attracted a
great deal of press coverage, Val d'Or was again constantly in the media
across the country. The town leaders were determined to prevent open-
air meetings and kept up a steady battle. Municipal authorities had enacted
a restrictive traffic bylaw to prevent "the Baptists" from presenting their
message to the people.

That summer a group of students from Central Baptist Seminary, Toronto,
who felt called to French ministry, came to spend a few months in northwestern Quebec. Their time was spent in intensive language study, practical
field training and making history alongside established missionaries.

Almost every week from August to the end of October, the Val d'Or
police stopped and imprisoned believers for conducting open-air services.
Those arrested included pastors and their wives, seminary personnel and

students, as well as men and women from local churches. Many Christians far from Val d'Or became concerned by the town's determined efforts to stop the preaching of the gospel. An unknown number of God's people prayed for victory in this situation and many came from outside the area to participate in open-air meetings, braving the serious outcome.

The Baptist Broadcast of August 14, 1950, translates the mood:

> The missionaries and Christians of North-West Quebec today are passing through the darkest and most critical hours in the history of our French evangelization. The enemy has come in like a flood. If we stop our work in Val d'Or the repercussions will be felt in La Sarre and Rouyn. The fresh opposition in La Sarre has come undoubtedly with the news that missionaries were successfully imprisoned in Val d'Or....If we take a backward step anywhere now our entire work will suffer. All our work stands or falls together. We are firmly convinced that this must be the hour of complete victory or crushing defeat. Our future ministry in the years to come in Quebec and indeed eventually in all Canada depends on the battle that now has been set. If it means months of imprisonment for God's people or indeed if blood must be shed in defense of this glorious gospel, it is our conviction that we must go on.

I too was eager to lend a hand in the open-air preaching in Val d'Or. Consequently, I served two prison sentences amounting to four months behind bars, the first starting in August, and the second at the end of October.

Prisoner becomes frantic

During my time in prison, I wrote this letter to my church in Noranda detailing one particularly intense incident:

> We had a rather strange experience while awaiting trial in Val d'Or. Late Saturday night they brought a man into the cells who had been drinking a little. A strange terror came over him, that terror that sometimes grips people when they are locked in small quarters. In turn he would scream and swear and weep. He would back down the tiny corridor, then run and throw himself against the wooden bars with all his might. He was a well-built young man and made the whole building shake as he threw himself again and again against the bars. Not content

with this, in his frenzy he went into the washroom, tore out the sink, breaking off the pipes and bringing the water pouring into the cells. Mr. Cloutier and I were on the bunk about four feet from the door and could see him come staggering down the tiny, dimly lit corridor with the sink over his head. He sent it crashing again and again with terrible force against the wooden bars until he had reduced it to a thousand pieces. It was a terrible sight to see this young man wading through the rising water cursing and screaming and sending pipe and porcelain flying in every direction. For two and one-half hours he continued, with the police helpless to do a thing. Finally he wore himself out and lay down in a cell and went to sleep. We could not help but think of those who reject the Lord Jesus and some day shall be locked eternally in that place where there will be weeping and wailing and gnashing of teeth and worst of all there shall be no rest day and night for ever and ever. For this reason the message of the gospel is so urgent and we must pray and give and suffer together that these lost souls might be freed from their sin by the power of the Lord Jesus.

In some ways those days behind bars were long and uncomfortable. The facilities were sparse; most rooms consisted of hard steel doors and cold gray walls. The food was also very poor. Thin gray porridge or pigs' feet frequently appeared on the menu. Before meals we said grace, "Lord, help us to get it down and keep it down"!

We especially prayed for God to give victory in Val d'Or and enable us to return to normal life. Yet, our stays in prison enabled us to give out copies of God's Word to prisoners and guards alike. What a privilege it was to have long discussions with these needy souls and point them to Jesus Christ.

After a number of days in jail, my brother Lorne and I were called to see the governor of the prison who was quite upset that so many prisoners were reading the Bible. He had granted us permission to have Bibles to read, but wanted us to understand they were for our personal use. He did not want Bibles given to any other prisoners. He warned us that if other prisoners were found reading the Bible, he would remove all copies from the prison.

When we informed other prisoners of this threat, far from discouraging them, it only increased their desire to read the Scriptures. New Testaments and Bibles were hidden under mattresses and kept away from the eyes of the guards. The Word of God continued to be read in private with greater intensity and urgency.

The midnight guard

One particular guard was of special concern to all of us. He worked the midnight shift, so we only saw him for a brief time before he went home in the morning. He appeared to be an extremely unhappy individual. He never smiled or showed any interest in hearing about the Lord Jesus Christ.

As the number of Christians behind bars increased, we were transferred to a lower cellblock where we occupied a whole section of the prison. One evening when I was still awake past midnight, I heard the rattle of keys in the door of our section and saw the surly midnight guard coming in. He had removed his shoes and was walking softly in his stocking feet. I watched him go down the line of beds where Christians were sleeping and wake Maurice Boillat, a professor of French from Central Baptist Seminary, who had spent the summer evangelizing with us. The guard told him to go to the washroom at the end of the corridor where the light shone all night.

I soon went to sleep, but was awakened at about 2:30 in the morning by Lorne who told me that Maurice was in the washroom with the guard. Just as I was explaining to my brother that they had gone in there about two hours earlier, Maurice and the guard came out. Maurice climbed into his cot and the guard left quickly.

We were burning with curiosity to know what the guard and Maurice had talked about. The next morning we learned that our cheerless guard was from a Christian home in Switzerland. He had rebelled against the gospel and his parents, and left his country to come to Quebec. He had mistakenly thought he'd never encounter Christians again, especially in a Quebec prison. He had been overwhelmed to discover that even here, God's people surrounded him. We rejoiced in that he now wanted to open his heart to the Lord.

Many months later, I was thrilled to see the midnight guard coming through the crowd as I preached in downtown Rouyn. He crossed the street and stood beside me, sharing my hymnal and singing with us the wonderful old hymn, "Come to the Saviour, make no delay, here in His Word He has shown us the way."

Thus in the midst of a long and bitter battle for the preaching of the gospel in Val d'Or, the Lord gave us special moments of encouragement. The conflict with town authorities lasted until 1954. By this time the Lord's servants who helped in Val d'Or had collectively spent a total of more than seven years in prison.

Victory in Val d'Or

My brother Lorne spent more than a year behind bars willingly facing opposition to win the right to proclaim the gospel freely. In July 1954, Noranda Baptist Church's newsletter reported the victory under the title: "Preach In Val d'Or Open-Air Unmolested":

> It appears now that the town council has left it in the hands of the chief of police to decide whether there is any obstruction to the traffic, stating that they have no power to prevent the holding of an open-air meeting in any public place so long as it does not impede traffic within the limits of the town.
>
> This attitude of the town council is almost a complete reversal of the decision they have handed down again and again over a period of almost five years when they flatly forbade any preaching anywhere in Val d'Or streets. The chief of police in turn is so willing and anxious to co-operate that he even suggested to the council that benches be provided on the sidewalk so that people could sit and enjoy the service better!
>
> The proof of the chief of police's attitude was seen in a great Saturday night open-air meeting in downtown Val d'Or last week, when dozens of people stood quietly along the sidewalks for nearly an hour drinking in the glorious message of the Gospel without any interference whatsoever from the town authorities.

I have told but a small part of the story of Val d'Or where my brother Lorne ministered for over 30 years, before moving to the Montreal area to pastor a French Baptist church in Verdun. He has started to write his own memoirs which will include many more details of what the Lord has done throughout his life and ministry.

People stirred to pray

We were almost to the point of despair many times during those long years of opposition. In the midst of the constant struggle, a number of people wondered if we should keep on. Some suggested we should follow the biblical command to turn away, "shaking the dust from our feet." But it was evident to many of us that this verse did not apply to Quebec, as thousands of French Canadians were hungry for the Word of God and ready to respond to its message. We persevered because the Word of the Lord tells us that it is our responsibility to take the gospel to a lost humanity even if it involves such experiences as we read about in the book of Acts. And because we saw God use our difficult circumstances for the advancement of his kingdom we continued to press on.

Gradually, as the people of northwestern Quebec accepted our presence in their midst, tolerance and willingness to listen increased. The public began to realize that we were sincerely preaching the message of the gospel and that we would continue our work regardless of their tactics to discourage us. One man in authority reputedly said, "We do not know what to do with these Baptists. They just keep coming back and don't defend themselves."

The news coverage we received brought the need of Quebec's millions to the attention of countless Christians and led them to pray. From church history it can be seen that the Lord's unchanging plans to accomplish his work have always been through the prayers of his people and the persecution we endured resulted in this very thing.

In the years since, as I have presented the challenge of Quebec as a mission field numerous times across our nation, I have heard the testimony of many people who told me how they read or heard the press reports of our difficulties and began to intercede regularly for this province. No sacrifice is too great, if the result is to enlist people to enter into the spiritual battle through the ministry of prayer.

10

Georgia—a true love story

Who can find a virtuous wife?
For her worth is far above rubies.
The heart of her husband safely trusts her.
Proverbs 31:10,11a

The first time I saw the girl who was to become my wife, she was just 15 years of age. In April 1945, I arrived for my first summer internship in northwestern Quebec and was met at the train station by two deacons from Noranda Baptist Church. The deacons then noticed two teenage girls from the congregation hanging around the station and called them over to meet me. One of those girls was Georgia Dalzell.*

Georgie's version of this event is somewhat more exciting. She went down to the train station with one of her girlfriends to sneak a peek at the young summer pastor. The girls were mortified when they were seen by the deacons and frightfully embarrassed, yet secretly thrilled, to shake hands with me. Georgie tells me she returned home in a daydream, vowing never to wash her hand again.

That first summer I noticed that Georgie was a committed Christian, as well as a pretty girl with dimples, but she seemed very young. In any case, seminary students were warned never to date girls within their church and I had every intention of following this sound advice. At this point in my life I was focused on ministry and girls were not a priority.

Two years later, in 1947, I moved to Noranda permanently. By then Georgie was 17 years old and a high school graduate. She was working at the mine's laboratory to save money to attend nursing school the following year. I noticed that she was still as pretty and much more mature.

---

* Georgia was called "Georgie" by everyone in the Dalzell family and it became her name among the Herons after her marriage to Murray.

Georgie had been born in 1929 in Detroit, Michigan, but grew up in Ottawa where her father was a cabinet-maker, a construction worker, and a milkman. He took whatever odd job he could to provide for his family during the depression years. In 1937, the family moved to Rouyn where the mining industry was in development. Georgie's paternal grandfather, Samuel Dalzell, was a big man with red hair, born in 1861 in Belfast, Ireland, where he had preached on the streets as a young man. He emigrated to Canada and continued to be an outspoken Christian, even serving some jail time for preaching on street corners in Ottawa in the 1930s. The family attended Metropolitan Tabernacle while living in the nation's capital.

Georgie accepted Christ as her Saviour at eight years of age and was baptized two years later by Noranda Baptist's founding pastor, Stanley Wellington. Her dedication to the Lord was evident from the start. She persevered through adverse circumstances even when it was difficult to take a stand in front of her schoolmates, and she brought unsaved friends to children's meetings after school. Georgie attended all the church meetings, including three on Sundays (Sunday school was in the afternoon). She would walk one mile each way from her home in Rouyn. She did this even through the winter months when the temperature sometimes plummeted to 40 degrees below zero.

During 1947 and 1948, we saw each other at church meetings and on outings with the youth group. Then in the summer of 1948, the young people spent a day together at Les and Jo Barnhart's cottage. Although I had never spoken of my growing interest in Georgie to anyone and treated her the same as the rest of the group, apparently Mrs. Barnhart had detected my sentiments. To Georgie's surprise and delight, Mrs. Barnhart took her aside to tell her to be more friendly toward me because I was in love with her.

That fall, Georgie left Quebec for a three-year nursing program at Soldier's Memorial Hospital in Orillia, Ontario. I had pictures from the day at the cottage, which served as a good excuse to write to her. It was the beginning of a long correspondence between us. The next time I had a speaking engagement in Ontario I stopped in to visit her. This was to be the pattern of our courtship for the next three years.

Georgie's nursing program imposed a rigorous schedule that ran from 7 A.M. to 7 P.M., seven days a week with only half a day off, and two weeks' holiday during the year. She managed to attend Orillia's Baptist church on Sunday evenings by running down to the service in her nurse's uniform as soon as she got off her shift at 7 P.M.

From the outset of our correspondence, her fellow students identified me as her "boyfriend." As news of my numerous incidents with the authorities was reported in the media, she was teased mercilessly about "Murray the jailbird."

Murray and Georgia Heron on their wedding day, May 27, 1952.

Or she was greeted with "Hey Dalzell, your boyfriend's in prison again."

Nevertheless, our relationship progressed and we soon wrote to each other every day, except if I was in prison. Then I was only allowed to write to and receive mail from my immediate family. As paper was provided solely for this purpose, I sometimes tore open envelopes in which I had received mail to write a letter to Georgie. I would then ask a prisoner who was being released from jail to mail it to her.

In the spring of 1950, after preaching in Ottawa I took a bus to Orillia and asked Georgie to marry me. She hesitated to accept my proposal because she lacked Bible school training and did not feel qualified to become a pastor's wife. But our deep love for each other won out and we felt led to join our lives together for God's service. Georgie graduated from nursing school in May 1951, and we made our engagement public when I gave her a ring in the fall of the same year.

We were married on May 27, 1952, in the little white Baptist church in Noranda. I was confident that Georgie was God's choice for me as a life's partner, and the ensuing years have confirmed it as we have weathered the ups and downs of life together. We enjoy so much the privilege of living and working together. God has used her in marvellous ways and she continues to be a true helpmate at my side. I especially value her as a prayer partner and appreciate her wise counsel on any number of issues.

Our life together

After several months of marriage, we were thrilled to learn that we would become parents. Although Georgie was quite sick during the pregnancy, time went swiftly as we prepared for the new arrival in our home.

Two weeks before her due date, Georgie noticed that the baby had stopped moving. Women from the church tried to reassure her saying this sometimes happens because the baby is constricted by lack of space. But she sensed something was wrong.

I remember clearly the day of her final visit to the doctor before the birth of our first child. At 4 p.m. I was in my study at the church when Georgie arrived with her heart-breaking news. The doctor had found no heartbeat and could only conclude that the baby had died. This was a dark hour of bitter disappointment, and tears flowed as the hopes of all those months were suddenly dashed to pieces. We were devastated and shocked, never having imagined this turn of events.

At the hospital, Georgie shared a room with an unsaved woman who was also grieving the loss of her baby. They talked and supported one another. Georgie saw God's hand in the choice of her roommate, it served as a gentle reminder that she had the privilege of knowing the Lord and had his comfort to help her through her sorrow. We decided to call the little girl we lost "Grace," as a tribute to God's abundant grace that saw us through this first severe trial of our married life.

The next hour of difficulty followed swiftly after the death of our little

The Heron family on the occasion of Isabel's wedding in June 1951. From left: Arnold, Harold, Earl, Murray, Isabel, Lorne, George and Ross. Foreground: Pearl and William Heron.

one. Only a few days after Georgie's release from hospital, she bravely consented to come to an open-air meeting in La Sarre. But we never reached the meeting, as our car was involved in a serious accident. Georgie was hospitalized again, this time for a badly broken knee. Others travelling with us in the car were also seriously injured and I suffered a concussion which caused me to black out for a period of four hours.

This was not to be the end of our trials. Disappointment followed again the next year when Georgie had a miscarriage. Although these were difficult experiences, they have enabled us to console and empathize with many people in similar circumstances throughout our ministry. The Lord has used Georgie, in particular, to counsel many women with compassion and sensitivity in this area.

Our children arrive

Our loving Lord in his great goodness led us through those days of testing and sorrow. In September 1955, we were overjoyed to become the proud parents of a healthy baby girl, Susan. The Lord continued to bless us exceedingly and abundantly, as just 17 months later another baby daughter, Joanne, arrived on the scene. Our only son, Donald, was born the following year. Then the next year, Georgie gave birth to our third daughter,

Janice. In just four years the Lord had entrusted four little ones to our care. And four years later, Carolyn's arrival completed the family circle.

Our children were a source of great joy to us as they grew up in Noranda where they received their elementary and high school education. In those busy early years, they participated in every aspect of our ministry. They stood with us in the stormy days of street preaching, used their musical talents on our telecast, and were a tremendous help in the development and operation of our youth camp.

Today they are happily married, living in different areas across Ontario and Quebec. They have given us 11 wonderful grandchildren, seven boys and four girls.

Our testimony is that of the psalmist who wrote:

> Behold, children *are* a heritage from the Lord,
> The fruit of the womb *is His* reward.
> Like arrows in the hand of a warrior,
> So *are* the children of one's youth.
> Happy *is* the man who has his quiver full of them.
> (Psalm 127:3–5a)

Pitfalls of the French language

The following story is a favourite of both Georgie and my family. It happened decades ago but still continues to elicit laughs. French is a difficult language and even after years of living in Quebec we still made mistakes.

In the 1960s I bought a clothes dryer from the Eaton's store in downtown Rouyn. Months later, the dryer broke down and I went back to the store to see the manager who was a personal friend of mine. I explained to him that my *sechoir* wasn't working properly. I was completely oblivious that *sechoir* refers to a hair dryer and that I should have said *secheuse*.

Not realizing my error, the manager graciously said, "I will have to look in my files to see when you bought it." Two minutes later he returned to say that he had no record of my having bought a *sechoir*. I told him emphatically that I most certainly had and that it now needed to be repaired. He was very patient and politely asked me to bring it back to the store so it could be returned to the manufacturer.

I left the store wondering how I was going to get the clothes dryer into the store. At that time we had a truck we used for camp. I enlisted the help of Réal Goulet, a young man then living at our house. Together we detached the dryer, hauled it out of the basement through my office, past the family recreation room and up the stairs. We put it in the back of the truck, drove all the way down Main Street and parked behind Eaton's.

I went in to tell the manager that I had the *sechoir* in the back of the truck. He looked at me quite mystified and said, "What?" Then he suddenly realized my mistake and said, "Oh you mean a *secheuse*!" I said, "Of course." I sheepishly returned home with my dryer to wait for a repairman. Georgie and the whole family had a good laugh, and this embarrassing episode soon turned into one of my best stories.

11

Children put out of school

But Jesus said, "Let the little children come to Me,
and do not forbid them; for of such is the
kingdom of heaven."
Matthew 19:14

A major challenge that arose early in the ministry among French
Canadians was the issue of schooling for the children of new converts. In
the 1950s, Quebec's French educational system was entirely under the
control of the Roman Catholic Church. Religious orders administered and
taught in the schools. Specific school hours were designated for the study
of the Roman Catholic catechism, and students were taken to parish
churches regularly for confession and religious ceremonies.

After deciding to follow the Lord, parents became concerned for their
children's spiritual welfare and were hesitant to send them to schools
where they were constantly exposed to Roman Catholic influence.
Furthermore, the children themselves often became the targets of taunts
and hostility from fellow students and teachers opposed to those who
embraced a "strange new religion." At that time the Catholic Church
authorities forbade its followers to read the Bible and were extremely pro-
tective of their position of power in society.

The wrong commandments

One Christian family that we knew continued to send their three school-
aged girls to the Catholic-run public school. One day the students were
asked to write out the commandments of the Lord as homework. When
their parents heard about the assignment, the father promptly took out his
Bible and had his daughters copy out the ten commandments word for
word from Exodus 20:1–17.

At school the next day, the girls handed in their homework. The nun teaching the class wanted to know where they had found so many commandments because the official Catholic catechism taught only four. The girls explained that they had copied them precisely as they were written in the Bible. Then without hesitation, the teacher closed their books, told them to go home and never come back to school.

A few days later this Christian family received word from the government that their family allowance benefits were being discontinued because their children no longer attended school. I heard the story when the confused parents came to see me, asking for advice.

There were Protestant school boards in the province, but at the time they operated only English schools. Concerned Christian parents were ready to send their children to English institutions but the school in Rouyn had established a policy not to accept French-speaking children on the grounds that an influx of children with no knowledge of English would be too difficult for the teaching staff.

In other towns, some English schools accepted French-speaking children but students were often set back, sometimes several grades, while they learned English. Depending on the age of the children, acquiring the necessary language skills was sometimes quite difficult and some students had trouble coping and catching up.

This left Christian parents in a real quandary. Every door seemed closed. Our church felt an increasing responsibility to these families, and we felt compelled to consider providing appropriate education for the children. Yet working out all the details of running a private school loomed as an enormous task. We would need desks, blackboards, books, educational aids and a place to operate the school. That was in addition to the challenge of finding a dedicated and qualified French-speaking teacher and paying his or her salary.

Once again, the Lord sovereignly did it all. Our first year of operation was 1950. The basement of the English church became a classroom for students of all ages and the large back yard served as a playground. In various ways, the Lord provided for all the furniture and equipment to operate the school. He also sent us valiant teachers from near and far. It was a missionary endeavour with all the attendant challenges. Some teachers had the additional task of learning French. Lack of French textbooks and teaching material greatly complicated the situation. Teachers often had to create their own curriculum or translate English books as best they could. What a blessing to God's people were the following women who taught at the school in Noranda for the ten years of its existence: Annette (Trudel) Gariepy, Margaret (Campbell) Heron, Mildred (Ford) Stallmach, Josie Bury and Hélène Malboeuf.

Teacher Josie Bury with French language day school students in Noranda Baptist Church.

Free transportation provided

During this period Mr. and Mrs. Hould, who had thirteen children, came to know the Lord and he accomplished a wonderful work of transformation in their lives. Immediately after their conversion, they realized that it would be unwise for their children to continue attending public school. Our school was in operation and ready to receive them, but they faced a costly transportation problem because they lived some distance from the church and had previously had free school transportation for their children.

The father, Roger Hould, worked at the local copper mine and his large family already stretched his financial resources to the limit. City bus fare for his school-aged children was an added cost that he could ill afford, but he was convinced he had to make this sacrifice for his family. A few months after the Hould children joined our school, I received a telephone call from the secretary of the Roman Catholic School Board. He was aware that the

Some of the many students who passed through the doors of Noranda Baptist Church in the 1950s.

Houlds were attending our school and paying for their own transportation. He announced that although the school commission could not furnish a school bus for the children, they would provide city bus tickets for the whole family. I was simply to make a list of the children who needed transportation and they would supply enough tickets to last until the end of the school year.

God's timing was impeccable. Just a week before this unexpected telephone call, the Hould family had felt convicted to give ten percent of their income to the Lord's work. They had just learned about the blessing of giving to the church and this was an extremely big step of faith for them. They took it after considerable soul-searching and despite the limits of their personal finances. When they learned of God's gracious provision of school transportation for their children, they were overwhelmed with gratitude as this represented a larger amount than their offering.

The Lord faithful to the end

We were grateful that the Lord had enabled us to provide a good education for the children of those who took a bold stand for Christ during the 1950s. Over the ten years of our school's operation, Quebec's education system gradually changed till it was no longer in the hands of the Roman Catholic Church. Like the rest of Quebec society, schools slowly became more accepting of different religions and cultures.

Once more it was inspiring to see the Lord step in to show us his power and faithfulness in building his church.

12

Full-time French ministry

Your ears shall hear a word behind you, saying,
"This is the way, walk in it."
Isaiah 30:21a

Following 12 years of growth at the Noranda Church, I felt God leading me toward a change. After much prayer, I saw that the time had come for the French and English congregations to go their separate ways. Although the joint work enjoyed harmony and blessings, both churches had reached a plateau because I had run out of hours in my day to lead and nurture the two flocks.

Weekly church activities kept both the English and French congregations and myself very busy. On Saturday nights we produced two television programs, one in English and one in French. The next morning, we aired two Sunday morning radio programs, one in each language. Then our church activities began with a Sunday morning Bible school in English followed by a worship service. After lunch our French congregation had an afternoon Bible School and an evangelistic meeting. Early Sunday evenings the English-speaking people met again for an evangelistic outreach. During the summer months, Sundays concluded with an open-air service in downtown Rouyn. During the week there were also prayer and youth group meetings in French and English, as well as regular visits in people's homes.

After investing over a decade of devotion and energy into these two ministries, it was difficult to make a choice. The Lord had used the support and vision of the English congregation to begin the French work, but now I saw that both groups would benefit from having their own pastor. In November 1958, therefore, I submitted my resignation to the English church.

I thus became the pastor of a small group of French-speaking Christians who were zealous for the Lord but young in the faith. Although they did their best, the congregation was not able to cover my salary as the English church had done. We stepped out in faith and the Lord gave us the joy of trusting him to take care of our material needs.

That same fall, the Fellowship of Evangelical Baptist Churches in Canada formed the French Canada Mission Board to oversee evangelism and church planting among French Canadians. This new board invited us to join them. Under their umbrella we appealed to Fellowship churches outside of Quebec to raise our financial support.

When Campbell Baptist Church in Windsor, Ontario, learned of our new French ministry, they immediately undertook to provide our full salary, which they designated to us through the head office of the Fellowship of Evangelical Baptist Churches in Canada. Once again the Lord had a ready answer for us, clearly demonstrating his approval and provision.

As God prepared me for full-time French ministry, he raised up John and Audrey Roberts from Ontario to carry on the ministry of the English church. The two sister churches continued to enjoy a united and effective testimony in the growing cities of Rouyn-Noranda.

Began in banquet hall

There were only 26 believers when we formed the French Baptist Church in Rouyn—just a handful of God's children with the burden of reaching the lost around us. It was a challenging hour. We were so sure the Lord wanted us to start a French church and move our meetings to Sunday mornings that we made our decision before we had found a place to meet. As I reflect on it now, it seems we lacked a great deal of wisdom to boldly launch out with nowhere to go.

Once again the Lord took the weak instruments that we were and blessed us despite our shortcomings. The week before our first meeting we still did not have a meeting place and we sensed the urgency of finding facilities. We went downtown to see a hotelkeeper who had an empty hall that we could possibly use. He told us that the place we suggested could not be ready for Sunday, but he did have another room that might serve our purposes. He led us through the bar to a beautiful and spacious banquet hall with a wall of windows overlooking the lake. It was a lovely room complete with chairs, a piano, and a telephone line to link us up with the radio station to broadcast our service.

The hotelkeeper offered us the use of this facility free of charge but for only one Sunday. We were thrilled nonetheless, as it was already Thursday by the time these arrangements were made and we had just enough time to contact all our people to tell them where our new church would be born.

This former Anglican Church, in the heart of the twin cities of Rouyn-Noranda, became Noranda Baptist Church. Murray Heron had begun this full-time French ministry in 1958 and the congregation had reached sufficient size to warrant larger facilities.

That Sunday morning more than 40 people filed through the bar, where patrons were already buying drinks, to attend our first French service as a separate church. We sensed God's blessing on our new venture as we worshipped the Lord in this unexpected place. The radio station transmitted a live broadcast of our meeting, free of charge. As an extra bonus all the people in the bar also heard the good news of the gospel.

From school to community centre

The week after our first meeting the Lord answered our prayers for facilities. My father-in-law, George Dalzell, who was the building superintendent of two Protestant schools in the city, helped us obtain permission to rent comfortable quarters in an elementary school for our Sunday services.

Some time later, we returned to see the friendly hotelkeeper to explore the possibility of purchasing a former community hall he owned. The one-story building was vacant and in need of considerable renovations but the location was ideal. It was in the heart of the community, just across the street from the city hall and fire department. Moreover, the price was within our reach.

The purchase energized our young congregation and everyone participated in cleaning, painting and renovating the premises. We put in a baptistery and the bar at the back became a nursery. Then a big sign went up on the front of the building. Now everybody knew that the French Baptist Church was there to stay.

Better yet to come

The church prospered in our new facilities. People came to Christ and followed him in the waters of baptism. We were quite content with our building even though it had no basement and the old, wooden structure was not very attractive. Yet a few years later the Lord showed us that he had something better in store for us.

A beautiful brick building in the heart of the twin cities of Rouyn-Noranda became available. It had been an Anglican Church, whose English-speaking congregation had dwindled, and the remaining few felt that it was time to let a French-speaking group use the building. It far surpassed our expectations. The facilities came with oak pews, a complete basement, a kitchen, space for classrooms and even a tall steeple tower with a bell.

The Anglican bishop gave us excellent terms and graciously allowed us to move in before we made our first payment. We had a great time of celebration with over 100 people gathered for the opening service. We joyfully rang the bell high up in the steeple to invite people to come and hear the Word of God.

13

Crowds hear the Gospel

For He shall give His angels charge over you,
To keep you in all your ways.
They shall bear you up in *their* hands.
Psalm 91:11,12a

After our hard-won battle to gain the legal freedom to preach in the open air, it was a joy to be able to go out and tell the wonderful story of the gospel without the threat of police interference. Although people were spiritually hungry and many wanted to listen, there were always those whom the Bible describes as "lewd fellows of the baser sort" (Acts 17:5, KJV), who came to disturb and destroy the meetings. But time and time again, we saw how God is able to undertake in every situation.

Motorcycle disturbance

One particular Sunday night, we had just begun the service in front of a gathering crowd when a young man drove up on a motorcycle. The motorcyclist stopped just two feet away from me and roared the engine as loud as he could to drown us out. Unexpectedly, a piece of his brand new vehicle then fell off right at my feet. The young man became very upset. He picked up the broken piece, swung his motorcycle around and drove off as fast as he could.

In his frustration he probably did not look where he was going and he ran right into a big fellow walking down the street with his girlfriend. This fellow punched the motorcyclist in the face and sent his glasses sliding across the sidewalk. Increasingly agitated, he picked them up, left quickly and was not seen again. Although unpleasant, this incident with the motorcyclist almost doubled the crowd that evening. People listened intently until we practically had no more voice with which to speak.

After the meeting I drove some church members home that lived in the country. About an hour later as I was returning home along Main Street, I noticed many people still gathered at the place of our open-air meeting. At first I thought there had been an accident, but then I saw young people from our church talking to inquiring university students. I stopped to listen for a few moments but realized that our young Christians were doing an excellent job on their own, so I went home.

About midnight that same evening, I heard a loud noise outside my house. Peering out the window, I saw a 1929 Model A Ford stopping on the street and several youths getting out. The young people from our church had stayed on the street all evening discussing spiritual matters. Finally the police had advised them to close the meeting. The inquirers wanted to stay longer but our young people suggested it might be preferable to go to the pastor's house. Thus, we had an influx of visitors in our kitchen, who stayed until one o'clock in the morning.

Growing interest

Our message was new to the majority of our listeners, and they were anxious to know what Baptists had to say. However, we feared that as the gospel became more familiar, people would not be so eager to stop and attend to the preaching. We were wrong. As the summers came and went, we saw an increasing number of listeners with greater concern for their relationship with God than ever before.

Many times we noticed that the most inquiring minds and hungry hearts belonged to young people of university age. The Lord continued to give us assurance of his presence and approval of this ministry in spite of many difficult situations.

On a Sunday night in August 1956, we saw one of the largest and most interested crowds we had ever known in nine years of open-air preaching in Quebec. Some 300 people filled the sidewalks and listened from parked cars and open apartment windows above the street. As the meeting progressed, it became increasingly difficult to carry on because two or three young men did everything possible to disturb us.

Just as one of the men was badgering the preacher, a city police cruiser arrived. The constable immediately arrested the man and took him to the police station. God gave us great joy in being able to conclude the service peacefully. Many needy souls listened quietly to the message that night and then those who wanted to learn more about eternity received a New Testament.

At our open-air meeting the following Sunday evening, the young man who had disturbed us the previous week returned, but this time to apologize. In front of all his friends, he begged us to forgive him for his misbehaviour and solemnly promised not to carry on in such a fashion again.

A smouldering cigarette

Another time, upon returning home from a Sunday night open-air meeting I noticed the smell of tobacco smoke as I entered the house. I asked my wife if we had had any visitors that evening, but just as she answered that we had not, my suit coat suddenly burst into flames.

Evidently someone had put a lighted cigarette into my pocket while I was preaching. Completely unaware, I had continued to speak and conduct the service while the cigarette smouldered in my pocket.

This incident became another illustration of God's providence for us. We had just returned from vacation and while we were away, visitors from Cleveland, Ohio, had stayed at our house. They had given me a beautiful new suit, just the colour and style I liked, one that fitted me perfectly. I was delighted that they had made such a wise choice but could not understand why they had done it. Now, with my suit completely ruined, I knew that God in his marvellous wisdom had once again anticipated my every need.

Hungry hearts

The Baptist Broadcast from the Noranda Church in June 1968 recounts the following events:

> It was a typical Quebec street service. Scores of spiritually needy French-Canadian young people were there. They listened to the preaching and singing; the evident hunger in their lives was seen at the close of the meeting. They would not go home. There were all sorts of questions they wanted answered. It was an unusual after-service as many young people came inquiring.
>
> Our Christian youth were ready to meet the challenge. There were half a dozen meeting at once as mixed-up teenagers swarmed around young believers to find the answer to their spiritual problems. One French-Canadian girl said, "I want a change in my life. I'd like to come here and discuss the needs of my soul."
>
> During the meeting, a Christian teenager, Bill Mikelait, was ruthlessly struck in the face. A rough young fellow seeking to

trip him up on his Christian testimony and wanting to see if he
practiced what he preached asked him what he would do if
someone hit him. The young Christian replied that he would
do nothing. His assailant promptly struck him three times
across the face. Bill later testified that it was not easy for him to
stand and take this without resisting.

A handful of pepper

On another occasion, a young man was giving me a great deal of trouble
during an open-air meeting. He pestered me by making annoying com-
ments, pulling my Bible from my hand, grabbing my tie and hanging
medals of the virgin Mary on my coat buttons. I was so distracted by this
troublesome young intruder that I did not notice another person
approaching with a huge handful of pepper which he threw in my eyes.
It was possibly the only time in my life that I stopped a sermon in
mid-sentence.

I was momentarily blinded and had to be led away. The first young
man who had given me so much trouble was suddenly touched by my
predicament. He ran into a restaurant and came out with a wet towel. It
was a moving spectacle for the crowd to watch this young man, previously my chief assailant, now with his arm around me, wiping the pepper
from my eyes.

Blind man comes to salvation

Our church newsletter, *The Baptist Broadcast*, from May 1969, tells the
story of a man who first heard the gospel at one of our street meetings.

> In a Sunday morning service at Emmanuel French Baptist
> Church a few weeks ago, a blind man made his way down the
> aisle to publicly confess the Lord Jesus Christ as his Saviour.
> This elderly French Canadian was first contacted at a tumul-
> tuous Sunday night open-air service in downtown Rouyn,
> where he was drawn by the sound of the meeting and stayed
> to hear the Word of God. It is wonderful now to see his spir-
> itual growth as he attends every meeting, leads in public
> prayer and witnesses to friends still away from the Lord.
> Although his physical sight is gone, his spiritual understand-
> ing is as a shining light that shines more and more until the
> perfect day.

Murray Heron was often found preaching in the open-air on the streets of Rouyn in the 1960s.

An invisible hand

In 1995, we met a man who told us he had tried to stop one of our open-air meetings approximately 30 years earlier. His story proved to us, yet again, the grace of the Lord in protecting his servants. During a meeting, this man drove his motorcycle toward us at full speed with the intention of knocking us down. As he sped toward us, he told us that he felt an invisible hand holding him back.

Later he spent time in jail and while there, he was constantly haunted by that experience. He was so deeply touched by this strange event that when he was released from prison, he went directly to the Baptist Church in Val d'Or. This tough biker then gave his heart to Christ and is now a living testimony to the power of God to change a troubled life.

Test of our faith

Open-air preaching in Rouyn was not only effective for reaching crowds but it was also an excellent opportunity to strengthen and develop new believers. Every week, the majority of our church members came to stand with us for what were often difficult meetings. From week to week it was impossible to predict what might happen.

One Sunday night a strong, well-built man pushed his way through the gathered crowd and told me to stop the meeting immediately and leave. I told him that we had permission from the authorities to preach on the street and I could see no reason to stop. He became belligerent and insisted that I stop preaching. When I refused to comply, he said he would return in ten minutes with others and take whatever means necessary to stop me.

Within a short time he came back, seething with anger. We wondered what he would do to move us. During this tense moment of anticipation two of our young men, Réal Goulet and Arnold Boulianne, moved toward him and told him to leave me alone. To our great relief, he looked into the determined faces of these two men of God and ceased to threaten us. As he left, he warned that he would return the next week with a gang to chase us away.

Before the open-air meeting the following Sunday night, I informed the Christians of the threats of violence we had received the previous week. I suggested that if anyone were not ready to be beaten and offer no resistance it would be better not to come. Regardless of these unpleasant possibilities, no one refused to participate. God honoured our actions by giving us a quiet, undisturbed meeting. The Lord had put his people to the test and given us victory by using adverse times to strengthen us.

A real training ground

Open-air meetings also served as a training ground for young French Canadians wanting to serve the Lord in the area of evangelism. Many unsaved high school and university students came to our meetings. Afterwards they approached us with countless questions about God and the Bible. Christian young people were driven to search the Scriptures, memorize verses and seek the wisdom of the Lord to deal with these inquiries.

Street meetings were also an ideal school for learning to preach. Far from the seminary classrooms and homiletics professors, would-be preachers gained precious practical experience. It was essential to speak in such a way as to draw the crowds and retain their attention. The feedback was immediate: if the sermon became dull and uninteresting the young preacher could soon find himself preaching to a lamp post or a fire hydrant.

An experience for the youth

It was our custom to begin our open-air ministry each spring on Victoria Day weekend. On this weekend, English-speaking young people from northern Ontario and northwestern Quebec would come to our Christian camp near Rouyn for a retreat. The highlight of the weekend each year was their participation in a street meeting in Rouyn. The young people would pile into cars or a bus and travel the 30 miles to the city for this meeting.

For these young anglophones, it was a novel and exciting experience to be exposed to a noisy meeting attended by a large crowd of Quebeckers. Afterwards, the campers were usually reflective and solemn on their return trip. Back at the camp, the teenagers gathered around a blazing campfire, where many expressed their desire to serve the Lord more completely after witnessing such a meeting.

Steve Baxter, now a Fellowship Baptist pastor in Waterdown, Ontario, told me that a weekend he spent at this camp was a turning point in his Christian life. Seeing hungry souls listening to the message of eternal life at the Sunday night open-air meeting had touched him deeply and influenced his life's calling.

14

On wings of faith

But when He saw the multitudes,
He was moved with compassion for them.
Matthew 9:36a

We were thrilled to see the Lord open up a new avenue of evangelism in 1958 when Northern Radio built a powerful television station in Rouyn-Noranda. The possibility of penetrating every home in the entire area with the gospel message seemed akin to the armies of Israel moving into the promised land and, step by step, taking the cities, towns and villages for the glory of God. A 700-foot transmitter tower could take our message far beyond the range of our radio programs and also reach thousands of French homes in northern Ontario.

One day in the middle of the winter, I drove to the location outside the city where the tower was being constructed in sub-zero weather. I parked my car near the site and watched the men far up on the cold steel finishing the work. From the comfort of my car I prayed, "O Lord, make this towering antenna a pulpit upon which I may stand and tell all this needy area the good news of the gospel." Within a few weeks my prayer was answered.

It was an enormous challenge and a great step of faith for our small church to embark on this project. But we had sought God's direction and despite our meagre resources, we felt at peace to go ahead and sign a contract with the station. Although our church was excited by this new medium, we also felt the monumental responsibility of being the Lord's representatives and sharing his message with a myriad of viewers.

Our half-hour program was called *Sur les ailes de la foi* (On Wings of Faith). It aired during prime time on Saturday nights, the evening with the largest viewing audience, right before the hockey game. Ours was the first program on the new station. What a thrill it was to stand before the cameras for the first time to conduct our live telecast.

The Lord gave us this method of evangelism not only to reach a great number of people with the plan of salvation but also to help change the attitude of the entire population of the area toward the gospel and our ministry. We were transformed from despised Protestants, who deserved to go to jail for their beliefs, to recognized television personalities with a message of hope and life.

A survey of the viewing area revealed that approximately 75,000 people watched our program. This staggering number overwhelmed me when I realized that hardly a ballpark in the major leagues contained that many people.

Viewers respond

Repeatedly we saw the impact of this new facet of our ministry. I received a telephone call from a Roman Catholic priest, the chaplain of hundreds of teenagers in a secondary school in Rouyn, who told me he watched our television program. I was stunned when he proposed to bring his pupils to our church on a Monday afternoon to allow me to make a detailed presentation of our beliefs.

I will never forget when the bus drove up to Emmanuel Baptist Church with 40 young people, the Roman Catholic priest, a few teachers and a nun. The priest had chosen students from every class in the school to take notes on what I said to report back to each of their classes. For a half-hour I talked to this rare audience about the great doctrines of Scripture and then gave them another half-hour to ask questions. Only eternity will reveal the fruit from the seed sown on that Monday afternoon.

Some months later the Sister Superior of a Rouyn convent called me. She was also one of our regular viewers and expressed great appreciation for the hymns we sang. In fact the nuns in the convent enjoyed them so much, they asked for a copy of our hymnbook so the convent choir could learn some of our evangelical songs. Shortly after this conversation, two nuns came to pick up the hymnbook and also invite our family for supper at the convent. Thus our whole family, plus a few members of our Baptist church, enjoyed a delicious meal with a large company of nuns in the residence of this religious order.

Before gathering in the dining hall for dinner, we were asked to visit an adjoining residence of cloistered nuns, women who had taken a life-long vow never to step outside the convent. These nuns stood behind iron bars and talked to us. Then our children sang a gospel song as they listened from their place of confinement.

There is no doubt that we saw the Holy Spirit use the ministry of tele-

On the set of Sur les ailes de la foi *(On Wings of Faith), the CKRN-TV television ministry of Emmanuel French Baptist Church in Noranda-Rouyn. The show aired during prime time on Saturday nights. Pictured (left to right): E. Chartrand, Leila Whitcombe, W. S. Whitcombe, Murray Heron and Jean and Helen Hamelin.*

vision to reach many needy hearts in very unusual places. I was invited to speak to the student body and faculty of a Roman Catholic seminary in Rouyn, where 75 young men were studying for the priesthood. It was an impressive sight: the faculty of priests dressed in their long black robes seated in the front pew and their students filing in behind them. This was an unprecedented event in my life, and I really did not know what to expect or how to proceed. Fortunately, a student stood up and asked me to explain the difference between the Roman Catholic teaching and the Baptist "religion." This question established an open discussion that went right to the heart of the matter. Throughout the evening, I sensed the presence of the Lord as we discussed and reasoned together about the great truths of justification by faith, salvation through confessing our sins to Christ, and the joy of having the assurance of going directly to heaven when we die.

There was no spirit of controversy but just a sincere desire to know what we believed. The Lord had evidently prepared the hearts of clergy and students alike as previous misunderstandings and prejudices had been swept away through our television ministry.

At a coffee break during the evening, students crowded around me and continued to ply me with questions. They requested another occasion to meet with me. I arranged for these aspiring priests to join our young people's group for their Bible study, where once again they heard truths from the Word of God.

The impact of the television ministry was far greater than we ever expected. I recall reading an account of a speech given by the Minister of Agriculture in a Roman Catholic parish hall during an election campaign. To drive home his point the Minister said: "As you heard on the recent Saturday night television program, *Sur les ailes de la foi...*" Although his quote was far from accurate, the fact that he used the name of our program in the hope of gaining popularity with his French-speaking constituents was evidence that we were respected and had a wide audience.

On countless occasions, when we were in public, whether in a store, a restaurant, on the street or at a public function, strangers approached us to say they watched our television program.

Viewers come to church

One Sunday morning, a new family I had never seen before attended our church. At the conclusion of the meeting, I invited people to come forward to confess Christ as their Saviour. The teenage daughter of this visiting family immediately responded and came down the aisle. As I counselled her after the service, I expected that she would need further explanations about the plan of salvation, but to my surprise she said she knew the message of the gospel. She told me how she had knelt in her living room and asked the Lord to save her at the end of our television program just the night before.

Another viewer, greatly moved by the message, began to come to church with some members of his family. The first one of the family to accept the Lord was 14-year-old Réal Goulet, saved at our youth camp in Val d'Or. Réal soon became active in the Rouyn church, and God later called him to ministry. He completed his theological studies at Central Baptist Seminary in Toronto and today pastors a French Fellowship church in the Laurentians.

Simple programs

We sensed the need to produce high quality programs to represent the King of Kings and yet we believed that simplicity and clarity were the best ways to reach the hearts and understanding of the entire population. We followed a format similar to our radio program line-up. Years of radio experience and open-air preaching made the transition to television fairly easy.

Music played an important part and we typically had several musical numbers in each program. Through the years, God provided many talented musicians for the broadcast. Christian singers from different areas of Quebec responded to our need and came to help.

Several singing groups made musical contributions. A fine group from Val d'Or organized by Margaret Heron, the wife of my brother Lorne, participated repeatedly, as did a group of young people from Noranda. Our own children sang many times when they were young and as part of the group from Noranda as teenagers.

Jean and Helen Hamelin frequently sang duets to open our program. Jean met Helen Hall at Bethel Bible school in Lennoxville, and they were married in 1956. Then from 1957 to 1967, Jean pastored churches in Malartic and Amos and was my assistant in Rouyn-Noranda. In addition to their contribution to the television ministry, the Hamelins helped out in open-air meetings, and were faithful workers at our camp. For a period of time, we also enjoyed the involvement of Jim Dorion, a local high school teacher who was an accomplished pianist. He had previous television experience, playing for the Canadian Broadcasting Corporation (CBC).

We packed as much as we could into each half-hour program. Typically we included a brief testimony or interview with someone whose life had been changed by the grace of God. This never failed to arouse interest. We also knew that many children would be sitting in the audience, so we always prepared a children's corner to touch the youngest hearts. As well, we reserved time to open the Scriptures, stand behind the pulpit the station had built for us and clearly explain the way of salvation.

The studio personnel were very co-operative and interested in making the program a success. They changed the decor if we requested it or made suggestions to improve the quality of production. When we planned a special program to promote our youth and children's camps, the staff provided a large realistic background of a beautiful lake. They even went into the woods to cut down trees to add to the set and created a very natural-looking campfire without real flames.

During the telecast a group of young people sat around the "fire" with Bibles and musical instruments, singing and giving testimonies. The overall effect was so successful that many viewers thought the program had been filmed at the camp. As a result of this single program, people from across the whole region with no connection to our churches brought their children to the camp.

God provides funding

As our church expanded into expensive avenues of service, one of the recurring questions was, "How will this be funded?" We believed that if something were a need, the Lord would provide, regardless of the cost. Our faith in this matter was based on a simple promise in Philippians 4:19, "And my God shall supply all your need according to His riches in glory by Christ Jesus." The church alone was far too small to carry the financial load of all its evangelistic ministries. Therefore, we made it a matter of special prayer to discern God's leading for us concerning new opportunities and fund-raising.

We felt strongly that God wanted us to do his work without appealing directly to our listeners for money. Rather, we saw it as our responsibility to inform God's people of what the Lord was doing and let him lead Christians to respond to the challenge of covering the costs.

Over many, many years, we experienced God's ongoing provision. The thousands of dollars needed to carry on the television ministry arrived month after month. Some individuals we did not know or had never met heard about our work and contributed regularly. Others gave considerable sums of money on a one-time basis. The riches of our heavenly Father never ceased to astound us. He also provided abundantly by bringing our needs to the attention of a wealthy Christian foundation based in Toronto. The group of men in charge of this foundation prayed for God to show them how to use the millions of dollars at their disposal. A Baptist pastor, who was a personal friend of mine and deeply concerned for Quebec's spiritual needs, was also a close friend of the foundation administrators. He suggested that they consider Quebec.

The foundation then sent a representative for a weekend visit to our church. He took back such a glowing report that this group wrote asking us to have Northern Radio send all our invoices for both radio and television to them. In this manner, God lifted a tremendous financial load from our small church. For a number of years, we had the blessing of using the facilities of four radio stations plus a powerful television outlet without ever seeing a bill.

Sur les ailes de la foi aired on a regular basis for almost 20 years but terminated when I left the Rouyn-Noranda area in 1977. Even today, over 20 years after our final broadcast, people still approach us in different areas of Quebec to tell us that they once watched our program, proving the truth of the words in Ecclesiastes 11:1: "Cast your bread upon the waters, For you will find it after many days."

15

A sanctuary in the wilderness

And He said to them, "Come aside by yourselves
to a deserted place and rest a while."
Mark 6:31

In the early 1960s, the Lord led us to establish a camp in northwestern Quebec. Those of us working to plant French churches in this area envisioned the camp fulfilling purposes of edification and evangelism especially in the lives of young people. We felt that new believers needed sound Bible training and an opportunity to see real Christian living in action. We were convinced God could use camps to help prepare future generations for ministry.

As this vision grew, the churches of Noranda and Val d'Or teamed up to conduct youth camps. Our first 10-day camp took place in 1961 at the Scouts' facilities in Rouyn-Noranda and the second year in Val d'Or. This ministry was such a blessing that we prayed for our own facilities to enable us to operate a more extensive ministry.

We explored several different areas to find a suitable location. Finally we discovered a beautiful piece of property on Lake Opasatica approximately 35 miles from Rouyn-Noranda that belonged to the Department of Lands and Forests. We went to the authorities at the local office in Rouyn and spoke to the engineer responsible. He willingly consented to negotiate a lease with us and make special arrangements because we were a church.

At first he proposed allotting us 200 feet of waterfront on the 20-mile-long lake, which was twice the amount normally given for private cottages. After expressing our deep appreciation for his help, we dared to ask for 1,000 feet of beach. He was taken aback and informed us that their office had never in their history granted that much footage. He could not personally approve it, but suggested we approach the head of the department.

Together, we went to see the person in charge. This man began by saying he was delighted to meet me, as he was a regular viewer of our television program. When I explained our reasons for requesting 1,000 feet of waterfront, he was in complete agreement with us and immediately told the engineer to write out a contract. In addition, he instructed him to reserve another 500 feet south and north of the leased property to prevent anyone from building too close.

The next day I met a government engineer at the camp location. Together we measured out 2,000 feet of beautiful lake beach. When the time came to plant a wooden stake to indicate the location of our property, the engineer wondered what name he should write on it. He also frequently watched our television program and asked if he could write the title of our program: *Sur les ailes de la foi.*

As he drove the stake into the sandy soil on the shores of that pristine lake, I looked up through the towering trees of the virgin forest and reflected on this fitting name. Certainly, if this undeveloped place was to be transformed into a camp where young people could come to eat, sleep, play, fellowship, and hear the Word of God, it was going to be accomplished "on wings of faith" and not in our own strength.

The policy of the Quebec Government was to lease undeveloped land to prevent speculation. A lease normally granted individuals 132 feet of waterfront for $30 a year with an option to buy the property at a very reasonable price once buildings were constructed. In our case, our contract stated that we could develop and use our large piece of property for a total cost of $25 for a ten-year period! It was also agreed that after the first ten-year term, we could renew the lease for another ten years at the same price or purchase the property outright at a minimal cost.

Although the local Department of Lands and Forests had approved our application for property in the fall of 1962, we still had to wait another six months or so before receiving final approval from the provincial office. By the summer of 1963, we were ready to begin hewing out a sanctuary in the wilderness.

The wilderness transformed

After the thrill of seeing God answer our prayers for a camp through the co-operation of the Quebec authorities, we now faced the daunting task of turning this virgin forest into a camp for the glory of God. The only people who had trod this property before us were the Algonquin Indians who had used it as a campsite many years before. The name Opasatica is actually an Algonquin word meaning "where the poplars grow." So we named the facilities "Camp Opasatica."

A government road stopped at the edge of our property. After that, it was only a tangled mass of thick underbrush and tall trees. At first the job seemed far beyond our human capacities, but it soon became an opportunity to see the Lord at work each step of the way.

Roger Jolin, a fine young Christian who lived nearby and who owned a huge earth-moving tractor, said he would be happy to help. I met him at the camp-site early one morning. He sat perched on top of his giant piece of equipment as I explained that we needed a road through the bush to the top of the hill where we wanted to clear land for a dining hall, chapel and parking lot.

He was very confident and even suggested that in half an hour I would be able to drive in. I watched dumbfounded as he went to work, clearing the forest and toppling trees. As he predicted, within a short time, I drove my car up the hill to the heart of our property.

Another man, Roland Loyer, who lived 100 miles away, offered to come in with men and equipment to complete the road with loads of sand and gravel. We had not foreseen this need, but God had. Roland arrived with a front-end loader and a truck. Soon we had a solid road for any kind of weather without it costing us a cent!

During the summer of 1963, we constructed a large building to serve as chapel and dining room. Camp Opasatica was not ready in time to receive overnight campers the first year, so we organized a six-day camp at the Scout's site in Val d'Or as we had the year before. However, we did use our new camp for day outings on a few occasions. On Labour Day, a hundred English and French Christians from the area came for a corn roast and regional rally.

The Lord is in the details

Time and time again it was wonderful to see God provide workers and materials from a variety of sources. In addition to our main building, there were soon spacious sleeping cabins nestled among the trees to accommodate campers. The Noranda Protestant School Board learned of our camp development and wanted to help. When they replaced playground equipment, the camp received their used apparatus that was still in excellent condition, providing many hours of pleasure for young campers.

My youngest brother Earl was an avid fisherman and excited to learn that our camp was situated on the edge of a lake full of fish. At the beginning of the camp's development he came with a lovely aluminum boat and motor to spend a few days fishing. He returned home to the Toronto area with a good catch of fish and left his boat and motor as a gift to the camp.

My brother-in-law, Bruce Hisey, also from the Toronto area, learned that we were beginning a camp without electric power. Bruce came to solve our problem. He towed an old Mercedes-Benz with a diesel engine all the way from Toronto. The car was rusted out but the motor was still in fine condition.

He parked the car in a little cabin in the center of the camp. He installed a powerful generator in the back seat and hooked it up to the drive shaft. The installation was really quite simple. Once we had wired the camp buildings all we had to do was start up the engine and let out the clutch to provide electric power to the whole camp. This set-up kept the camp running smoothly until Hydro Quebec finally installed a power line many years later.

In the early stages of development, Arnold, another one of my brothers, came to help. To his delight, he discovered a spring of cold, fresh water oozing up through the sand at the edge of the lake. He immediately found a shovel and started digging. In no time, he was up to his knees in fresh bubbling water. We quickly built a wooden box around him to keep the sand from caving in.

Thus in one afternoon, we had a well that was sufficient to supply the entire camp with an unlimited quantity of water. We covered the well and installed a pump to take the water where we wanted it.

Arnold was so enthusiastic about the new-found spring that he had gone into the water with his clothes on and had not taken the time to remove his wallet from his pocket. Later on, the clothesline behind the dining hall became the center of attraction. Arnold had hung his money out to dry. Now everybody knew how much my brother was worth!

Many people contributed time and effort to the camp. Murray Sandell was one such individual. He was a high school history teacher in Noranda and had a burden for young people. He helped to develop the camp and arranged many youth activities. The young people remembered one of his special projects with great amusement. He organized a group of young people to remove the numerous stones from the beach by carefully piling them into the boat and then moving the cargo into deep water and throwing the stones overboard.

After a number of trips back and forth, the task became a little tedious. Murray suggested they could make the unloading part easier by simply tipping the boat over and letting the stones fall out. But as the valiant crew tipped the rock-filled boat, it filled with water and sank 35 feet to the bottom of the lake.

At first we thought we would never see that boat again but later we found a solution to our problem. We had a professional diver come, dive into the depths and lift out the stones. After a few hours, our lovely boat drifted slowly back to the surface. We were then able to continue enjoying the boat and a beach free of stones.

Fiery trial

In our second year, we constructed a chalet close to the lake that quickly became a favourite spot on the property. It had a spacious living room with a fireplace and a large window looking out over the water. We enjoyed this cozy meeting place for staff prayer meetings, Bible studies, fellowship and planning sessions. But in the fall of the year it was built, it was completely destroyed by fire. I stood beside the smoldering ashes of that building and wondered how this waste could possibly fit into the Lord's plan.

God showed us that what seemed at first like a disaster can be used for his glory. A Christian in the Noranda Church had a barn filled with building materials that he had accumulated for years with the intention of building a big, beautiful home. Just when we needed it, this man changed his plans and gave us his supplies.

In this unexpected way, the Lord provided us with a large quantity of dry lumber of every shape and size, windows, doors, roofing tile and all that was necessary for a much larger building than the chalet we had lost. We used the materials provided to erect a new dining hall, so meals no longer had to be served in the chapel.

When the Quebec Department of Lands and Forests heard of the fire and our plans to put up a bigger building, they generously gave us a large addition to our existing property without any extra cost.

Crushed by snow

Some years later, we had the bitter disappointment of finding the camp chapel completely crushed by the weight of accumulated snow when we went to inspect the camp in the spring. The chapel had been constructed to withstand the normal weather conditions of northwestern Quebec. The man in charge of the project had put up round arches that extended from the floor on one side of the building to the floor on the other and the roof was covered with sheets of aluminum. This slippery surface was intended to prevent the snow from accumulating. The structure held up for several years, but that year the snow was particularly wet and sticky and it evidently piled up on the roof and brought down the building.

Once again the Lord showed us that he could use an apparent setback to move his purposes forward. Upon reflection, we recognized that the original building had in fact become too small for our growing needs and the aluminum roof was a severe drawback when it rained, as the noise level made it almost impossible to carry on meetings.

Once again we went to work. The broken arches and twisted metal were removed and the floor was extended further out. Two big picture windows were installed looking out toward the lake with a fireplace in the center. A steep cathedral ceiling was put into place to ensure no further snow accumulation. The Lord provided the necessary workers and materials. My brother Earl came with a team of men from his church. They arrived on a Friday and by Sunday the extra floor was down and the walls were in place. The windows and doors were installed and the big roof covered it all. It became a beautiful new building.

A safe bridge

Camp Opasatica could only be reached by crossing a wooden bridge over a narrow part of the lake. After a few years of use, the old bridge became weakened and unsafe for the busloads of campers and heavy trucks. We were concerned that a busload of campers might one day go through the bridge and down into the water.

Those of us running the camp realized that building a new, sturdier bridge was far beyond our means and our abilities. We saw that our only hope was to ask for the government's help. This possibility seemed extremely remote as there were no other developed properties in that area besides our camp.

As in everything else, we believed that the Lord was in charge and could provide for all our needs. We prayed and made an appointment to meet Camille Samson, our provincial member of parliament. When we explained our pressing need for the camp, he readily sympathized with our concern and wanted to help. While we sat in his office, he immediately telephoned Quebec City. We were a little mystified, wondering how long it would take to get the political machinery rolling. But after just a brief conversation, he hung up and simply said, "It has been approved. When do you want us to begin building the bridge?"

That same summer the government moved in with their heavy equipment, tore down the old bridge, drove steel pylons down to the rock at the bottom of the lake and built a solid bridge worth thousands of dollars. All we had to do was praise the Lord!

Looking back on blessings

After several years of hard work on the grounds, I stood on the sandy beach surveying the view. I thought back to the first day in 1962 when the engineer

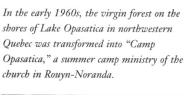

In the early 1960s, the virgin forest on the shores of Lake Opasatica in northwestern Quebec was transformed into "Camp Opasatica," a summer camp ministry of the church in Rouyn-Noranda.

had planted his surveyor's stake in this untouched wilderness. The surroundings were still beautiful but I could now see through the towering poplars to a beautiful dining room and kitchen complex 200 feet away.

To the right of the dining room and a little closer to shore was the chapel with big windows looking out over the lake. Here scores of campers heard the gospel while sitting in front of the big fireplace. Further to the right and even closer to the water was a special clearing in the woods, overlooking the lake below, where countless campfires were held. Dozens of young people had gathered here around the glowing embers of the campfire at sunset to testify and confess Christ.

When I looked far to the left, I could see the girls' cabins nestled among the trees on the far side of a small ravine. In these cabins counsellors had prayed and helped needy hearts early in the morning and sometimes late at night. The boys' cabins were located on the opposite side of the camp property. These buildings too had seen moments of spiritual victory.

My heart was filled with gratitude to God for the years of ministry on this property that had become a veritable sanctuary in the wilderness. Campers had come from a variety of backgrounds to this special place where all were able to hear the voice of the Master in the quietness of the great outdoors.

Eternal rewards

Besides the regular camping program there were also special occasions, such as a trip to town on a Sunday night to attend a tumultuous open-air meeting, or times when baptismal services took place beside the still waters of Lake Opasatica. The reason for the Lord's abundant blessing on this ministry was found in the words that the Quebec engineer had written years before on a piece of wood by the lake: "on wings of faith."

The October 1970 issue of our news bulletin, *The Baptist Broadcast*, recounts this moving scene of camp life:

> The campfire was burning low. The sun was almost gone in the western sky. A thousand stars were beginning to blink on in a cloudless night. Dozens of campers were slowly making their way to cabins among the trees. A teenage girl lingered behind.
>
> No definite invitation had been given but there was a burden on her heart. We sat down on an old log beside the smouldering embers. A soft summer moon was coming up over the lake a few feet away.
>
> In the quietness of the setting sun we talked about eternity, the faithfulness of God, His love for the lost, and the assurance of a home in Heaven. She prayed simply and clearly asking the Lord to forgive her sins and receive her as a child of Heaven.
>
> There was a deep reverence, a quiet joy, and assurance that a mighty God whose handiwork was all around had bent down, heard and answered. This was the first night of summer camping at Opasatica 1970.
>
> This is why the sweat and tears, disappointments and sacrifices of working with French Canadian youth at camp is worth it all— young lives changed for time and eternity.

16

Preaching across the nation

*...he told in detail those things which God had done
among the Gentiles through his ministry.*
Acts 21:19b

Despite a full ministry schedule at home, I often accepted speaking invitations far beyond the borders of Quebec. The extensive media coverage we had received during the stormy early years of our ministry had stirred up much interest among believers who were eager for first-hand information.

I spoke at local churches, missionary conferences, youth retreats, Christian camps, regional conferences and evangelistic meetings from coast to coast in Canada and in many areas of the United States. Sometimes I wondered what I was accomplishing on these long trips away from home. Was it wise to spend so much time far from my mission field?

Yet when I considered the big picture, it was obvious that in order to reach Quebec for Christ, we needed the involvement of English Canada as prayer partners and financial supporters. In those early years (and still today to a certain extent) our viability depended on their prayers, stability and support. I learned that talking about Quebec in a Vancouver church was possibly just as important in reaching French Canadians for Christ as a Saturday night television program in Rouyn-Noranda. Everywhere I went, I talked about the burning challenge of Quebec.

A key to victory—people pray

There is no doubt in my mind that the Lord poured out his blessing so powerfully in Quebec because a great number of people everywhere prayed for the province's vast spiritual needs. Prayer enables those far from the mission field to be effective partners with missionaries on the front lines. The Scriptures are clear that God's blessing is poured out when God's people intercede, and little is accomplished when there is little prayer.

This was the case when the Lord sent the children of Israel to conquer the Amalekites, as recorded in Exodus 17. Joshua was commanded to go to the battlefront with his men but God told Moses to carry the rod of the Lord to the top of a hill and raise his arms heavenward. To me this is a beautiful illustration of how the Lord accomplishes missionary work. Joshua and his men only had victory when Moses held his arms up. Whenever he let them down, the enemy prevailed against Joshua. The same is true of missionaries. I am convinced that it is impossible for missionaries to be successful on the field if God's people neglect to pray.

We also encouraged people to pray by sending frequent newsletters and bulletins regarding the work in Quebec. Over a number of years, our mailing list grew to include thousands of people from all over North America. We wrote detailed accounts of events and projects to stir our prayer partners to remember us constantly. Our first news bulletin was entitled *The Baptist Broadcast* and then when I went to work with SEMBEQ, our French seminary in Montreal, we called it, *Quebec Alive*.

Coming in the darkness of the storm

Christian camp ministries have always held a special place in my heart, and I count it a great privilege to have been invited to speak at a number of camps. I fondly recall Muskoka Baptist Conference (MBC) in Huntsville, Ontario. I was honoured to serve there as a conference speaker at adult conferences, youth and children's camps.

One occasion stands out in my memory. It was my first time as a speaker at a week-long teen camp at MBC. Almost every day, young people were making decisions for Christ. When we came to our last meeting, over 100 campers assembled in the old wooden chapel at sunset. There was much expectancy that at this closing service a number would make decisions for the Lord.

My young audience was attentive as I spoke. Just as I was finishing my message and announcing the closing invitational hymn, we heard the roll of thunder across the lake, and saw bolts of lightning flash through the chapel windows. Then the wind began to blow, the rain fell and the lights went out. Except for an occasional flash of lightning, the campers were sitting in total darkness waiting for instruction from me. I wanted to preserve the sacred atmosphere of this critical time of decision, so I prayed for clear direction from the Holy Spirit.

I knew that the campers had come with flashlights to light their way back to the cabins after the meeting so I said, "You all have your flashlights but I don't want anyone to turn on their light unless they want to make a decision right now for the Lord. If you want to confess Christ as your Saviour, turn on your flashlight, point it to the floor and come down the aisle to the front."

While the thunder rumbled and the lightning flared in the night sky, lights went on all over the room and began moving forward. We sang softly as young people made spiritual commitments that changed their future in this world and the next. Within a few minutes the electricity came back on, and we were thrilled to see a line of young people stretching from wall to wall across the front of the chapel. The end of this story can only be told in eternity.

The smoke changes direction

Another outstanding time was at Saugeen Bible Camp in the Georgian Bay area of Ontario where scores of teens had gathered for a week. Once again I had the joy of seeing the Holy Spirit touch young lives and bring them to Christ. However, in the midst of the blessings there was one cabin of girls that was very rebellious. All week long they created problems by not co-operating in any camp activities. This was especially difficult as the ringleader among the group was the daughter of a staff member.

On the final evening, we held a campfire service where campers were to testify of God's work in their lives. Usually this was a special and meaningful moment, but in this case the atmosphere was spoiled by the girls who refused to join us. Instead they sat in a little group about 50 feet away, out in the field, in the semi-darkness.

We proceeded with the campfire anyway, but then we heard the sound of pouring rain falling on the maple trees on the hillside behind us. In the gathering darkness the sound got closer and closer, and just as we thought we had to stop the meeting to avoid getting soaked, the wind suddenly changed direction. I watched the smoke curling up from the embers of the fire gradually shift from blowing south to straight up in the air and then in the opposite direction. We could hear the rain retreating over the trees, as if the Lord was saying, "I don't want you around here just now, I have work to do."

Everything was perfectly still and the fire continued to burn. Unexpectedly the group of girls sitting in the field got up, made a wide circle around the campfire and came to stand by the flames. The ringleader spoke first and then one after another all the girls followed, asking everyone to forgive them for the way they had acted all week. They publicly confessed that they wanted to accept Christ as Saviour. We saw how the Lord uses the wind, the clouds and the rain to do his eternal work.

A living room message

On another occasion I was able to speak to a chapel of campers at Sunnybrae Bible Camp high up in the Rocky Mountains without leaving the comfort of my living room in Quebec. The camp director had asked me to speak at their morning chapel via a telephone connected to the sound system at the camp. He had arranged for my phone to ring at 8 A.M. Eastern Standard Time, but since there was a three-hour time difference, the campers had to be seated in the meeting place by 5 A.M.

Over thousands of miles of telephone wire, I challenged them to consider the spiritual needs of Quebec and the province's lack of Christian workers. I urged them to give their lives to the Lord's service that he might use them in the place of his choosing.

Churches in America

I am also grateful that the Lord has allowed me to present the needs of Quebec to Christians in the United States who know so little about this neglected Canadian mission field. The Lord opened doors for meetings at missionary conferences in the New England states, Pennsylvania, Ohio, Tennessee and even Florida.

We have had great fellowship on a number of occasions with Michael and Michelle Kirby in Cleveland, Ohio. Mike heard an interview I did on the Moody Bible Institute Radio Network, which aired across the United States. He had felt the call to work among Roman Catholics in the Cleveland area, and when he listened to this interview on the radio, he was greatly encouraged by God's blessing on our ministry in Quebec.

He obtained my phone number and called, asking to meet with me. Sometime later I was able to visit him and his church in Cleveland, and this was the beginning of a great friendship. I have spoken to his congregation a number of times, and he has also visited Quebec with a group of men from his church.

Great blessings

I have great admiration and appreciation for the enormous weight of responsibility my wife, Georgie, has carried throughout our ministry. In addition to my busy schedule on the mission field at home, the numerous opportunities to speak in churches near and far meant that she often cared for our family alone. Georgie made the best of sometimes difficult circumstances and learned to draw her strength from the Lord. She has been

Murray and Georgia Heron celebrating their 45th wedding anniversary in 1997.

a model of patience and devotion.

Today, after more than 50 years in the province of Quebec, I can only come to the same conclusion with regard to my ministry. I still consider being used of God to usher souls into his family the greatest privilege a person can have. My calling to preach the gospel has been a constant source of blessing in my life.

Epilogue

Turning point and beyond

"Be strong and of good courage; do not be afraid,
nor be dismayed, for the Lord your God
is with you wherever you go."
Joshua 1:9b

Throughout the 1960s and into the 1970s, the Lord continued to bless our work in northwestern Quebec. He gave Georgie and me the stamina to keep up a variety of activities in addition to our regular church schedule, including our radio and television programs, open-air meetings, and our summer camp ministry.

The province of Quebec experienced sweeping changes in the 1960s. This once devoutly Roman Catholic society abandoned the church in vast numbers. Restless and disillusioned, a whole generation of young people began searching elsewhere for truth. We had the joy of seeing a good number of these young French Canadians dedicate their lives to serve the Lord. Some were called into vocational ministry.

In 1969 there were 19 French Baptist churches in Quebec associated with the Fellowship of Evangelical Baptist Churches in Canada. The years ahead would bring unprecedented growth in the number of believers and in the number of churches as the Lord continued to save French Canadians. In 1973, God led provincial leaders with a vision for the future to found a new, decentralized Baptist seminary known as SEMBEQ. This seminary represented a new approach in theological training, one that was based in the local church. This approach to theological education enabled a greater number of workers to prepare for ministry without leaving the province.

We were unaware that the Lord was also preparing us for a change. In the spring of 1974, we decided to drive down to Toronto to attend my niece's wedding. We enjoyed a relaxing drive through beautiful Ontario and looked forward to meeting family and friends at the outdoor ceremony.

As we travelled south in the first new car we had ever owned, we noticed that we were following a car from Ohio. Engraved on the license plate was a reminder to buckle up. Georgie responded by immediately fastening her seat belt. I did not fasten mine, as it was getting close to lunchtime and we were planning to stop. At that time there was no law that made it compulsory to use a seat belt.

Near Burks Falls in northern Ontario, a light rain began to fall. As we came to a hill, a woman driving a sports car came toward us in the passing lane. Suddenly she lost control, swerved in our direction and hit us almost head-on.

The massive impact pushed the engine of my new Ford into the front seat and pressed the steering wheel up against the back of the seat. Because I did not have my seat belt on, I was thrown sideways, out of the path of the steering wheel. Had I been held in place, I would undoubtedly have sustained a serious injury or been killed. As it was, my face was severely cut and bruised and I suffered a concussion.

For Georgie, God had used a license plate from Ohio to save her life. Her seat belt kept her from being thrown through the windshield. However, the force of the collision on her seat belt broke three of her ribs. She also suffered multiple cuts and bruises as well as a badly broken and lacerated ankle.

A serious car accident in 1974 proved to be a turning point in the Heron's lives.

We were both driven 100 miles by ambulance to Toronto General Hospital for medical treatment. Georgie was hospitalized for a month, whereas I was released after one week.

This accident brought us to an important turning point in our lives. We recovered slowly from our injuries and during convalescence it was impossible for us to carry out our normal workload in ministry. The Lord provided young people from our church to direct the summer camps that year, as we were not physically able to assume a demanding camp ministry.

My daughter told someone that I looked like a monster when I got home from Toronto upon my release from hospital. Just a few weeks after the accident, I did a television program while my face was still considerably swollen. I asked the program director if he could adjust the camera to minimize my injuries. After several valiant attempts he told me it was impossible and that I would have to tell viewers what had happened. Although we have long since completely recovered from this accident, the prolonged convalescence led us to reconsider our ministry in Rouyn. Soon the Lord guided us in a new direction. In the fall of 1977, we reluctantly left northwestern Quebec and the many activities that had consumed our lives for more than 30 years.

Our family moved 400 miles away to the city of Laval, just north of Montreal where I became the third pastor of the French Baptist church in Chomedey. I felt the privilege and saw the challenge that the Lord was placing before me as I answered the call to minister in this city of 300,000 souls, the second largest urban centre in the province.

Missionaries Weldon and Dorothy Clark founded the Chomedey church during the 1960s when the gospel was progressing very slowly in Quebec. Through perseverance and sacrifices, these faithful servants of the Lord and a small number of followers had managed to buy a well-located piece of property and erect a modest church building.

Then Pastor Jules Mailloux and his wife Lucie, a young Quebecois couple who had studied at Bethel Bible Institute in Lennoxville, Quebec, continued the work from 1971 to 1977. When we arrived, a new wind of church growth was already sweeping the province. God used the social upheavals of the Quiet Revolution to bring salvation to unprecedented numbers of francophones. All over the province, the prayers of God's people were answered and churches grew and multiplied as never before.

This was also the case in Laval. Soon the little church building became too small to accommodate the growing congregation. We sold the original place of worship, temporarily moved to a high school auditorium and purchased a future building site in the heart of the city.

Over the next nine years the Lord accomplished many wonderful things.

We witnessed the outpouring of God's grace on our adopted province and we saw him answer our prayers continually, as Quebeckers from all walks of life joined God's family.

As French churches grew and spawned daughter works in Quebec, the need for church and lay leaders increased. The Lord had uniquely prepared SEMBEQ, our French Baptist Seminary, and our regional church association to meet the demands of the day. Born out of necessity during this time of rapid growth, church leaders later saw how a church-based leadership-training program was closer to God's biblical mandate to reproduce themselves than the traditional seminary approach.

In 1986, the Lord led us to leave the Chomedey church to serve him with SEMBEQ alongside the seminary president, Jacques Alexanian. Although the seminary was into its second decade by then, there was a tremendous need to expand its operations and seek the financial and spiritual support of Christians outside the province. Our task was to travel thousands of miles across Canada and the U.S.A., visiting hundreds of churches to promote the school and encourage believers to continue to pray for Quebec. We did this for the next ten years as well as ministering-at-large in camps, retreats and churches.

We saw God continue to bless French churches with numerical growth and increased maturity. However, even though there are now over 70 Fellowship French Baptist churches, plus hundreds of other evangelical churches in the province, recent statistics reveal that less than .06% of Quebec's six million people are Evangelicals. The harvest has begun, but it is not over and workers are still needed in the Master's field.

Northwestern Quebec

The twin cities of Rouyn-Noranda now have a population of over 40,000 people. However, the ministry there has not grown like we have seen in other parts of Quebec. This region is in great need of prayer. Since our departure the vast majority of our former congregation has left the area and no one has been able to carry on the ministries of radio, television, open-air meetings or the camp.

We were concerned that the camp buildings and the equipment accumulated at Camp Opasatica did not go to waste after we left. Our desire was for it to continue to be used in the Lord's work. This is exactly what happened. A team of men from our association's camp in the Laurentians came to dismantle the chapel, the dining hall, the speakers' cottage, all the campers' cabins and even the storage shed. All this material was loaded on a flatbed truck and transported to *Camp des Bouleaux* near Mont Laurier.

Murray and Georgia surrounded by their children, spouses and grandchildren on the occasion of the Herons' 40th wedding anniversary in 1992.

There it was put to good use improving their facilities to meet growing demands and expand their ministry to churches in southern Quebec.

Only eternity will reveal the large number of people whose lives were touched and transformed by Jesus Christ during those years in northwestern Quebec. Although our first concern is not to look for visible results, it is tremendously encouraging to see people in ministry today who come from those years of difficult labour in northwestern Quebec.

Today we live in a suburb north of Montreal and continue to be involved in helping to plant churches. We have a particular burden for the vast Laurentian area that stretches for over a hundred miles north of us. In this vast recreational region, dotted with towns, villages and resorts, there are very few churches or Christians.

I believe that the great promise given to Joshua so long ago is still true today: "Every place that the sole of your foot will tread upon I have given you." (Joshua 1:3a) My prayer continues to be: "Dear Lord, leave your footprints across Quebec and claim these people for your own."

Appendix 1
Map of the province of Quebec

Appendix 2
Area of ministry (map detail)

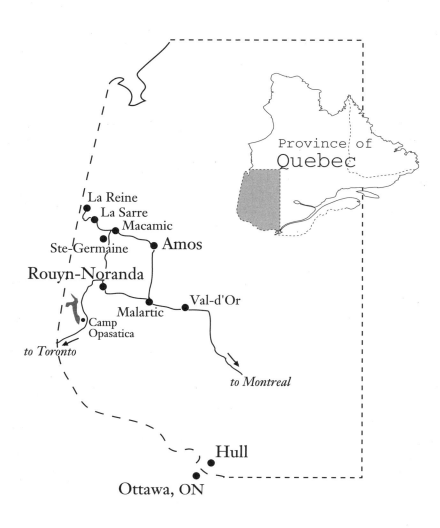

Province of
Quebec

La Reine
La Sarre
Macamic
Ste-Germaine
Amos
Rouyn-Noranda
Val-d'Or
Malartic
Camp
Opasatica
to Toronto
to Montreal
Hull
Ottawa, ON

Designed by Janice Van Eck
Set in ITC Dyadis and Janson Text
Printed by Hignell Book Printing, Winnipeg, Manitoba